The SUPERhero's Journey

A Maverick's Guide to Purpose, Impact and Legacy in a Complex World

J. H. Tepley

London, 2024

"You have an important role to play in the evolving destiny of the world. What will you choose it to be?"

"Never stray from the Way."
- Miyamoto Musashi

Published in the United Kingdom by ARIYA Verbum

www.newerasuperhero.com Contact: reachout@newerasuperhero.com

The Superhero's Journey by J. H. Tepley

© 2024 Jay H. Tepley. First Edition.

Jay H. Tepley asserts the moral right to be identified as the author of this work in accordance with the 1988 Designs and Copyrights Act.

All rights reserved. No portion of this work may be copied or transmitted in any form (electronic, photocopying, video or audio recording or otherwise) for commercial and media purposes without the prior written permission of the publisher.

This book may not be reproduced, resold or otherwise circulated through electronic or mechanical means with any alterations to the original cover, binding or content, including translations to other languages, without the publisher's prior consent.

Using small text samples and images is permissible for reviewing and quoting purposes, as well as non-commercial research and private study providing that the source is clearly stated.

This book's purpose is to give you clarity and actionable advice to help overcome and fend off depression. It is meant for inspiration purposes only, and not intended to be a substitute for medical care, professional counselling or therapy.

Join our community! Visit t.me/NewEraSuperhero

▼ LOVED THIS BOOK? Please share your thoughts on Amazon! Every voice counts. ◢

BY THE SAME AUTHOR

The Lightwatch Chronicles, Book 1: The Guardians

The Lightwatch Chronicles, Book 2: The Journey

High Purpose Code

Manifest Like A Pro

The Unbreakable Entrepreneur

Codex Semperis

The Elements of the Mind

The Mindgates Blueprint

What if You're NOT Depressed?

ARIYA Meditation Quotes

The Secrets of Warrior Willpower

CONTENTS

By The Same Author 7

Who Is This Book For 8

Chapter 1: Man's Search For Meaning................................. 11

Chapter 2: A Call To Adventure.. 19

Chapter 3: The Mentor.. 25

Chapter 4: Human Beans, or the Secret of Vertical Growth. 31

Chapter 5: Becoming a Tornado 43

Chapter 6: The Chosen One 57

Chapter 7: Acting 'Because', Not 'Because Of' 63

Chapter 8: A Deep Dive: Behind the Veil............................. 71

Chapter 9: The Courage To Be Yourself 81

Chapter 10: How Planes Fly: The 4 Forces of Flight in Self-Development 93

Chapter 11: Your Priorities Shape Your Life....................... 111

Chapter 12: The Broken Ikigai... 119

Chapter 13: Remembering Who You Are........................... 125

Chapter 14: The Man's Secret to Self-Realisation 131

Chapter 15: Transcending the Levels of Consciousness 143

Chapter 16: Unlocking Your God State 159

Chapter 17: Designing a Personal Manifesto 181

Afterword 203

One Last Thing 204

About The Author New Era Superhero: Self-Mastery & Service 205

Get Social! 207

THE SUPERHERO'S JOURNEY

WHO IS THIS BOOK FOR

If you want to learn what living your Purpose really means and how to get there -

If you feel like you've hit a plateau in your personal growth and looking for answers -

If you want a simple blueprint to navigate amongst the increasing complexity of the world -

- you're in the right place.

Inspired by the timeless framework of Plato's dialogues, this book offers an empowering and revolutionary way of thinking designed for success in both your business and personal life.

On the pages that follow, you can find crucial puzzle pieces to complete your roadmap to a deeper self-understanding – and an inspiration to unlock your divine potential and bring your service to the world to a new level.

This book may fascinate you, elevate your mindset, challenge your current paradigm, and prompt important questions and discoveries.

It can help you generate new ideas aligned with your greatest vision for your life, and support you on your mission.

It is a manifesto for the visionaries that aim high.

For rebels and adventurers.

For the curious and open-minded.

For those who are not here to fit in, but to blaze their own trail.

If that is you, welcome on board. I hope you'll enjoy your flight.

CHAPTER 1: MAN'S SEARCH FOR MEANING

"In the absence of purpose, life becomes an endless journey to nowhere."
- Seneca

Mike sat in his room staring at his laptop screen, frustrated. He could have easily finished that presentation in about 2 hours. He knew that. Now, a day before the deadline, he gazed mindlessly at a blank laptop screen and still procrastinated.

Finally, he grabbed his phone and opened Instagram. "Maybe a hit of dopamine will get me motivated," he lied to himself while scrolling past cats speaking Chinese, scantily clad influencers bending backwards by the poolside, and dull lead generation adverts with photos of guys posing with rented supercars and private jets.

Mike sighed, switched the screen off, put his phone back on

the desk and reclined in his high-back swivel chair. He was tired.

His business was doing well. He couldn't complain about his social life, either. And yet…

There was a strange growing sense of emptiness creeping in on him as days went by. It was like the world was slowly sliding into greyness. Things he used to enjoy lost their appeal and seemed more and more pointless. Even sending this presentation to the potential partners seemed pointless, somehow.

It was as though he was trapped in a reality he existed in, in a life he worked so hard to create. Now, merely in his thirties, he had the lifestyle many envied and aspired to. Once upon a time, he used to aspire to it himself.

But now, it just didn't excite him anymore.

Mike rubbed his temples looking at the ceiling.

'Is there a purpose to all this?' he mused, not for the first time. 'Most people live lives of quiet desperation,' a voice in his mind said. He couldn't recall who this quote was by, but it rang true.

He eyed an empty cup and a stack of books on the coffee table to his right. There were mostly investment books; and mostly because graphs and tables looked annoying on Kindle.

But there were also others. That book by Tony Robbins he picked up at some seminar but never finished. Some books on mediation. A best-selling book on finding one's life mission, which he found insufferably boring.

There were also a few that he liked. 'The Art of War' by

Sun Tzu with a fancy script printed in gold. A tattered copy of 'Meditations' by Marcus Aurelius. It was a mini edition, easy to carry in one's pocket, which Mike used to do quite a lot. 'Start with WHY' by Simon Sinek.

The last one served as a reminder.

Looking at the big red letters on the cover, Mike often asked himself what his true, deepest Why actually was.

Why was he doing this? Why did he even start this business?

Money?

Security?

Recognition?

Mike winced. Those reasons certainly were true when he first started. He wanted all of them.

But now, they seemed so petty and mundane.

He wanted to create a real difference, and a real impact, he thought.

For that, his current business didn't seem to be enough. Mike turned around in his chair.

He didn't know what else he could do. He even meditated every morning just like the gurus said. It didn't bring him any closer to the answer, though.

He turned the other way. A message notification popped up on the screen, but Mike ignored it. He was in no mood to chat right now.

'Come on,' he said to himself. 'Surely, there must be a way.

You're an entrepreneur. A problem solver.' He thought back to the many self-development seminars and bootcamps he went to. Most of them were just time-consuming pitches for the next product in the line, but some part of him sensed that the truth was somewhere there, near, and he could find it if he tried hard enough. 'Come on. There must be an answer.'

He looked through the window by his desk, at the gleaming towers of the skyscrapers. The spring wind rolled scattered scraps of clouds high above. Mike pensively drummed his fingers on the desk but then his eyes flashed. He remembered something.

Two days ago, his old friend Luke flew in for business, and they caught up for a few drinks in that quirky Japanese-themed bar that Mike liked.

As usual, the liquor-infused conversation flowed towards the old days, the business, the girlfriends, and their mutual love for airplanes. Mike toyed with the idea of getting a pilot licence one day.

It seemed to be a night like any other. But before they parted, Luke unexpectedly turned to Mike, studied his face with a tipsy concern and blurted out, "You need to *do something*, you know."

"Hmm? What are you on about?" Mike blinked at him, confused.

"You know what I mean," Luke insisted. "You need to sort

yourself out. You don't seem like your normal self these days."

"Oh, shut up."

"No, listen," his friend spoke again. "I'm serious. I don't know what's going on. but you seem to sound low all the time. Even worse, you pretend you're f-king okay. And I know you're f-king not."

"Shut up. Well… I don't know. Maybe," Mike admitted somewhat blurrily. "It's just… everything seems kinda pointless. Like some bad party, I can't wait to leave. I want to do something meaningful, you know? To be *someone*. Not just another guy who made a lot of money, bought a house and a Lambo, and f-king died! It sucks. Everything sucks." He sniffed angrily.

Luke beamed a sudden smile. "I know what you need," he announced, bringing the glass to his lips and taking a swallow.

"I'm not taking any drugs," Mike told him gruffly.

"That's not what I was going to say," Luke continued. He lowered his voice and leant forward to be heard through the music. "You need to find your purpose."

"Purpose, huh?" Mike sighed and looked away. "I've been thinking about it, actually," he admitted. "I even went to a seminar of that dude, what's-his-name… and the one by Tony Robbins." He snorted. "WikiHow has 13 easy steps!" He growled out of the blue then quaffed the rest of his drink and waved to the bartender to get another. "And guess what? Nothing. Nobody knows anything. They just want to sell me more stuff. I'm fed up with that."

"I know what you need," Luke grinned again.

"What f-king is that?" Mike threw at him, annoyed with his stupid smugness. "Oh, omniscient one."

"Get off," Luke snorted. "You don't do it that way. You need a *teacher*."

A girl in a cheap yukata showed up with a tray carrying two drinks. Mike angrily snatched his.

"A teacher, yeah?" He questioned Luke again. "Every f-cking YouTuber is a teacher these days."

"No, I mean a real one. Like a mentor. A sensei of sorts."

Mike squinted at him. "A sensei of sorts?"

"Yeah, someone who can actually do it."

"Someone who can actually do it," Mike repeated in a mocking high-pitched voice then looked at his friend wearily. "And where do I find one? Do you know anyone like that?"

Luke swirled his drink inside the glass, then looked at it through the light. He then shifted his gaze back to Mike, his eyes smug and mysterious.

"Maybe I do."

CHAPTER 2:
A CALL TO ADVENTURE

> *"You can't evolve into what you won't explore."*
> **– T.D Jakes**

Weird how some ideas can take root.

Mike told himself it was unlikely that Luke's drunken 'wisdom' could lead him to anything worthwhile. And yet the thought remained, buzzing like a wasp trapped in a jar, annoyingly consistent. It didn't help that it had stirred curiosity in him as well.

Before long, curiosity swamped everything.

'What do I have to lose?' Mike thought, finally giving in to the lure of an adventure. 'In the worst-case scenario, I'll get to check out a new part of the world. And if Luke's ideas hold any water, maybe I'll get some good pointers from that mentor dude.'

Mike has always been an action-taker.

Only a week later, he stood at the airport exit hailing a taxi, in the heat unusual for an early morning. All he had was a suitcase, the address and a hope.

Luke said that Sage (as he called the mentor) chose his students carefully and there was no way of knowing in advance if he would qualify. But also, if he did get accepted, his life would change forever.

The promise sounded cheesy, but something in Luke's voice made Mike believe that the enigmatic Sage might have the answers he was looking for.

After a short stop at the hotel, the taxi dropped him off by a modern house painted all white, surrounded by a neatly kept garden. Mike walked to the tall entrance door. The gravel on the curved pathway made him glad that he left his suitcase at the hotel.

The maid who opened the door enquired about the purpose of his visit, then nodded and him asked to wait before disappearing inside the house.

The entrance hall was also white, with a marble floor and a resplendence of white peonies in a large vase by the door. The only splash of colour was the long framed strip of silky fabric, bright orange with some Chinese calligraphy on it.

There was nothing unusual about the interior and yet it was imbued with an elusive yet powerful feeling of deep peace and something that Mike could only describe as 'sacredness'.

He stood in the hall looking at the calligraphy scroll, imagining the Sage to be an old Eastern master with a white beard and traditional clothes, a spitting image from the old kung fu movies he watched as a kid.

He turned to the sound of the opening door. From the further end of the hall, a young man walked springily to him, greeting Mike by his name. He wore a white shirt with a standing collar and a pair of grey high-fashion jeans.

"I'm here to meet Sage," Mike said.

"At your service," the man smiled and lightly bowed his head.

Mike looked at him, dumbfounded. "I mean, the actual Sage…?" He asked awkwardly.

"The actual one," the man confirmed.

Mike looked at him again, more carefully. The man's face and body looked like he was hardly in his twenties, but his eyes were wise and deep, and his hair was touched with silver.

"I…see," Mike muttered, eyeing the orange bracelet at Sage's wrist, the same colour as the calligraphy scroll behind him. "I see," he repeated with more composure. "Thank you for finding the time. I'm here to—" he cleared his throat, "I wanted to learn. About my Purpose. My friend said you could help."

"Possibly," Sage replied noncommittally. "But it comes at a cost."

"Money is not an issue."

"Very well. But that's only part of the equation. The real cost is the one you'd have to pay to yourself."

"I don't understand."

"Commitment," Sage explained. "Reaching your Purpose is not a done-for-you service. Think of it like getting fit. You can't just pay the gym owner then drop off your body at the gym and pick it up when ready."

Mike snorted. "Makes sense." He studied the Sage again. Nothing in his appearance was what he expected to see. The Balmain jeans least of all. *And why does he look like he's in his twenties?! Did I even get the right dude…?*

"Yes, you did," Sage replied to his thoughts out loud.

Mike gasped. "You can tell what other people think?!"

"Sometimes." Sage looked at him with warm nonchalance. "So, you said you wanted to learn?"

"Yes. And I hope you can accept me as a student."

"We'll see," Sage said. "Tell me, why do you want to find your Purpose?"

"Because," Mike's eyes lit up, "I always felt there must be something more to life. That I was meant for something greater. Some better, more exciting life. I don't want to just pay bills and die. I want to make a difference. I want to be someone people would look at and say, 'It was thanks to him that my life changed for the better'. To become someone who matters. So that my life has some real meaning to it. That's what living a purposeful life means to me, anyway."

"And why do you want all that?" Sage smiled somewhat elvishly. "What is your WHY?"

Mike gasped again. "That book!" He spattered. "It was on my desk... how did you know?"

"I've been doing my job for a long time," Sage said. "So anyway, what is your Why?"

Mike lapsed into silence. He realised he didn't know. He never asked himself that deeper question. Somehow, the surface-level motivation seemed enough.

"I... don't know," he was finally forced to admit.

"I understand that you meditate?" Sage asked in an affirmative tone of voice.

Mike nodded. "Yes."

"Well then, go and try to find the answer. Also, check with yourself if you're willing to pay the price. After that, we can talk again."

"Oh right, I forgot to ask, what is the price? How much?"

"The price is your whole life up until now."

"WHAT?!"

Sage gave him a knowing stare with a hint of irony. "If you

want to live your Purpose, you need to *become the person who can do it.* Your current self can't — so you will need to let go of this old version of yourself. To upgrade your mental OS, so to speak. From there, your new life will unfold."

"Doesn't sound too bad."

"Not all ideas, people and circumstances will be able to follow you into your new life," Sage warned. "It will be a very different version of reality to what you're living in now."

"Well, I'm not too happy with my life right now, anyway. I don't even feel pumped to work on my business anymore. I'd rather try something new."

Sage nodded. "Have a good think about it, and let me know. This is not a decision to be taken hastily. Once you start on your journey, there's no going back."

"Sounds a bit like the Matrix," Mike chuckled.

"Some things in movies are more real than you think."

CHAPTER 3: THE MENTOR

"What man actually needs is not a tensionless state but rather the striving and struggling for some goal worthy of him."
- Viktor Frankl

Mike spent he next day in his hotel room, mulling his options over and over. He even rescheduled the Zoom call with his team to have a clear space to think.

The image of the young dude in jeans didn't sit right with him. That's *not* what a "sage" is supposed to look like. Or dress like, for that matter. He didn't seem legit. Mike snorted to his thoughts. *Why did Luke hype him up so much?*

But then he suddenly remembered Sage reading his thoughts with disconcerting ease, there on the spot. And the unusual, deep expression in his eyes. 'Maybe I'm being too superficial,' Mike said to himself. 'Judging a book by its cover and all that… Hmm. I should try and do that homework, I guess.'

The homework did sound interesting.

"Right, let's give it a go," Mike sighed, sat down and closed his eyes. He learnt to meditate a while back but he was never really happy with his practice. No matter how he tried to motivate himself, sitting still and trying not to think was excruciatingly boring. He also never got any wonderful breakthroughs or insights other people spoke about. The meditation mostly served to calm him down. Although sometimes, that state of calmness brought some pretty good ideas.

After only two days, Mike was back at Sage's house, still puzzled and confused yet it felt like his legs had simply brought him there before he knew it.

"So, did you have the time to think?" Sage asked him.

"Yes! No…" Mike rubbed his face. "I mean, it doesn't matter. I should do it. My answer is yes. Can you help me get there quick?"

"I could," Sage said. "But you wouldn't benefit from it."

"Why?"

"Because fast gains don't last. Same goes for mind development."

"Gotcha," Mike clenched his fist and pensively considered the definition on his arm. "That's fair enough."

"The question is…" Sage measured him with a testing gaze, "Why do you reckon you should do it? It's a lot of work. You could just keep things as they are, you know. It'd be a lot easier."

"I don't care what's easier!" Mike looked Sage square in the eyes. They had an unusual colour of dark amber. "I guess you don't get it, but… Imagine going through your life just rotting away. Feeling useless. Feeling like your life is just passing by. Not being anyone or creating anything worth remembering. Just wasting your time here."

"But you've achieved a lot."

"But other people's standards – yes, maybe. But it just doesn't feel enough." For some reason, speaking about it made Mike angry with himself. He set his lips and looked down silently contemplating the white Gucci trainers Sage was wearing.

"I see," Sage said. "So you feel you're meant for something greater?"

Was that a trick question? Mike frowned.

Admitting that he always felt different somehow from other people around him and that he did, in fact, believe that there should be some special, greater mission in life that the universe had in store for him bordered on arrogance. It was true, however.

He studied Sage again. The expression on his face was calm and gentle, yet tinged with something else; irony, perhaps. It seemed like he knew the answer.

Mike shrugged. Fine.

"Yes," he answered simply. "You seem to know this already?"

"I do," Sage said. "Otherwise, you wouldn't have come here. There are plenty of distractions in the world for young people like you."

"Young?" Mike breathed out. "But you're young yourself!"

"I'll take it as a compliment." Sage smiled. "I'm a lot older than you think. Now, what about your Why?"

Mike glanced away, at the tall white door leading from the hallway inside the house. The door was closed. "Well…" he said uncertainly, "I did try to figure that out. The best answer I got was that my soul just naturally wants to go in that direction. It's like a pull. Hard to explain in words. An inner calling. I just know I *have* to do it."

Sage nodded. "And what would happen if you don't?"

Mike winced. He remembered an awful vision he saw once in his mind's eye, of a life so suffocatingly uninspiring, so empty, that it felt like being buried alive. A state that pushes people into an addiction or worse. The very thought of it brought a waft of depression. "I don't want to talk about it," he said in a heavy voice. "You probably know the answer anyway."

"I do. But it's important that you too are aware of it."

"I'm aware," Mike muttered glumly. He pressed his lips and looked at the Sage again. "So, what's the verdict?"

Instead of an answer, the Sage turned away and opened a glossy narrow cupboard by the door. He pulled out two long sticks that looked for all the world like a pair of lightsabers, and activated them. They flared up with the typical buzzing sound.

Mike watched his movements, speechless, shock gradually giving way to excitement.

"What… are you doing?" He finally blurted out, giving

Sage an unbelieving stare.

"Let's see how good you are," Sage told him elvishly, brandishing his lightsaber. He threw the other one to Mike. "Here, have a green one for the start."

Mike caught it mid-air and uncertainly took a defensive stance. But then, a vivid recollection swept over him like a nostalgic tide, whisking him back to his childhood days, where he and other boys would pick up sticks pretending them to be real swords. "Alright then." His eyes sparkled with mischief.

Mike grabbed the hilt with both hands and cut through the air with a swoosh.

"Not bad," Sage said. His first blow came in from the right, with some deliberation.

Surprising himself, Mike deftly parried the strike. But as soon as that, Sage's blade did a shining volta of cyan blue right before his face and landed upon Mike's left shoulder before he realised what was happening. Despite the speed, the touch was gentle like a tap.

Sage looked at him and a dangerous smile briefly touched his lips. "Not bad," he repeated putting his lightsaber down and deactivating it.

"So," Mike asked still befuddled by all this, "am I accepted then? Will I become a Jedi like my father?" He grinned.

Sage chuckled at his words. "We'll see. You certainly have what it takes."

CHAPTER 4: HUMAN BEANS, OR THE SECRET OF VERTICAL GROWTH

Mike spent hat night turning and tossing on his bed, unable to sleep. The logical part of his mind told him that everything that had happened was ridiculous: him listening to his tipsy friend, him travelling here, and his naive hope that the strange ageless dude would be able to help him, somehow.

Yet there was some other part of him, his soul maybe, that was excited at the opportunity to train with the mysterious lightsaber-wielding mentor.

"Come on," he said to himself, "surely I can at least try. No harm in trying." In response, his mind entertained him with the cornily famous 'There's no try' quote. Mike sniffed.

'Fine. Maybe I can just do it, then.'

'Would you really be OK with leaving your old life behind?' his mind played a devil's advocate.

Mike contemplated the possibility for a few moments.

'I guess I would,' he finally answered in his thoughts. 'Can't be much worse than it already is. And who knows, maybe it's actually going to be better. *A lot* better.' Something in him was certain of it, even though Mike couldn't explain, why.

He was at Sage's house at 2 o'clock sharp the next day.

He wasn't sure what to bring, so he brought it all – his laptop, his electronic notebook, and a regular paper notebook, just in case. He even put his nicest t-shirt on. A long-forgotten memory of his first job interview swam at him as he knocked on the door. Mike took a deep breath.

"Hello there," Sage greeted him with a broad smile. "Come in. Coffee upstairs."

"I keep meaning to ask. Does it mean anything?" Mike pointed at the now familiar calligraphy scroll as they walked past it.

"Yes," Sage replied. "It says Mujidō. 'The Timeless Way' in Japanese."

"You speak Japanese?!"

"I do."

Mike glanced at Sage with added respect. "Wow, that's impressive. And what's the Timeless Way?"

"You'll find out."

They entered a large bright room with floor-to-ceiling

windows, bathed in the afternoon sun. There was a sofa and some chairs, brilliantly white and aetherial against the round beige carpet. A small acrylic table with a holographic sheen stood in the middle.

On the wall behind them, Mike noticed another scroll - it looked like the one downstairs, only larger.

Sage gestured invitingly to the chairs. "Exploit the sitting furniture," he said, "while I organise our coffee." He pulled out his phone and texted someone.

"I would suggest taking notes by hand," he remarked, noticing the laptop in Mike's bag. "Qui scribit, bis legit."

"Hmm?"

"He who writes reads twice," Sage translated off-handedly. "Latin. An old habit."

Their coffee soon arrived delivered by a sporty dishevelled guy in his early twenties who didn't look like a maid. He carefully put the cups on the table.

A strange golden glow seemed to gleam over the coffee for a split second, just then, and was gone. Mike shook his head. It must have been a trick of the light.

"Thank you," Sage said to the assistant. "I see you blessed it properly this time?"

"I did!" The guy beamed a smile.

"Well done. It looks perfect," Sage told him.

"Thank you!" The guy smugly curved up his lips, then

looked at Mike and smiled a magician's smile. "Welcome," he said.

"Err…" Mike looked at him, confused. "Thank you?"

"Tanner is an apprentice," Sage said.

"I try," Tanner quipped. He ran his fingers through his dishevelled hair. "My best decision ever." He looked at Sage. "If there's nothing else, I'll go meditate in the garden."

"A great idea," Sage told him.

Tanner smiled, sharply put his arm across his chest and was gone.

Mike looked at Sage confounded. "Am I… also an apprentice now?"

"Not yet," Sage told him. "You'd need to learn quite a lot more before you can call yourself that."

What is going on… Mike crossed his arms on his chest contemplating if he made the right decision by coming here, after all.

Sage gave him an ironic stare. "Go ahead, voice it."

Mike rubbed the bridge of his nose. He pensively looked at the coffee in his cup. "This all seems strange," he said frankly. "That guy—"

"What about him?"

"He… I don't know. He seemed—" Mike chewed his lip— "he didn't seem normal."

"What do you mean?"

"I don't know how to put it... Just not like others. He seemed...otherworldly, I guess? I can't think of the right word."

Sage laughed. "Tanner will love it. I'll tell him you said that."

"No! Please don't. I didn't mean to—"

"It's alright," Sage told him calmly. "You wanted to find out about Purpose, didn't you?" He picked up his cup and took a swallow.

"Yes, I did. But..."

"Listen. Here's the first thing you need to know. It's what you saw in Tanner. Living your Purpose is never about horizontal development, only vertical."

"Hmm?"

"You know how you went to all those self-development trainings and seminars where they promised to teach you 'this one crazy trick' or 'this secret skill', 'or these three easy steps to success' but nothing ever happened?"

Mike grunted. "Yeah."

"This is what horizontal development is. You learn more skills, more tricks, more strategies – but you remain the same person as you were before. And because of that, you can't even use some of that knowledge fully. It's like downloading new apps on an outdated OS. They just become clutter that slows you down. Those skills may be unnecessary or not supported by your current 'mental OS' in the first place, and essentially turn into junkware."

"This…makes a ridiculous amount of sense. Why would they slow me down, though?"

"Because that extra knowledge solidifies your current ego story. And this is exactly what's keeping you trapped in a reality you don't enjoy. And you don't enjoy it because that's *not* how we were meant to live as human beings."

"Alright, so how were we meant to live?" Mike finally remembered about his coffee and took his cup. It was cold to the touch but the drink inside was still hot and aromatic as though it were just brewed. Mike took a sip and his eyebrows went up. It was the most delicious coffee he had tried in a long while.

"Vertical development." Sage smiled, noticing Mike's face. "Similar to how plants grow."

"I don't understand."

"Take coffee, for example. Consider the seed, the seedling, the young plant sprouting its first leaves and finally the grown-up coffee plant that produces the seeds for the cycle to repeat itself. They all look different. Some of these stages differ to the point that for someone who didn't know, they wouldn't even look like they belong to the same plant. And yet they do."

Mike rubbed his brow. He wasn't sure where Sage was going with all of this. Still, he dutifully made a note in his notebook.

"We are like that, too," Sage continued. "Imagine if the coffee beans were conscious, and had their own civilisation. In their civilisation, everyone would have to forever remain a seedling because the knowledge of how to become a fully grown plant was lost. And because of that, everyone would be plagued with the feeling of inadequacy. Like when something crucial was missing but they couldn't figure out what it was. So everyone just carried on, feeling depressed and stifled – because that's how you feel when your growth is hindered."

"That's exactly how I feel," Mike muttered while taking notes.

"Because we were not meant to spend all our life on one stage of development. We are human beans, you know."

Human beans. Mike wrote it down and circled the words. He liked the sense of growing clarity within. "So with humans, what would vertical development be like?"

"You' would evolve in your mind and become a more elite version of yourself. Having said that, as you grow, you become a different person altogether. Just like a mature coffee plant doesn't look anything like its seedling."

"Interesting. Who will I become, then?"

"We don't have words to describe what happens as we grow but… the closest description would be something like becoming a real-life superhero. Bending reality with your mind."

"Doing WHAT with my mind?!"

Sage smiled. "Didn't you want to be a superhero as a kid? Never once tried to move objects with your mind?"

"Of course!" Mike snorted. "Who didn't…"

"See?" Sage finished his coffee and added, "This is exactly why people resonate so strongly with the idea of superheroes, angels, demigods and such."

"Why?"

"Because deep down, they can sense the truth. We are supernatural beings at our core. Remembering that is the first step to unlocking your Purpose."

Mike rested his chin on his hand. "This sounds *way* out there," he admitted. What he heard shook his view of reality quite a bit. "Intriguing but way out there. Didn't expect to hear that."

"I know," Sage said calmly. "But it is what it is. You either grow or you remain trapped and stuck." His shirt was bright white against the blue sky in the window behind him. "You know why life seems so exciting at a younger age? Because we learn and grow at the same time. And we are happy – because this is our natural state. If you want to live your Purpose, this is where you start."

"Where?" Mike asked. "Just so I can write it down better."

"You start by realising that you can't step into your Purpose as you are now. Your Purpose is not what you do, but who you are. Once you grow into a greater version of yourself, your actions will naturally flow from there."

"My Purpose is not what I do but who I am?" Mike cocked his head to the side.

"Yes. Your Purpose is not a career choice. Setting up new businesses while staying internally the same is a lost game. They will just burn out after a while and leave you feeling empty."

Mike set his lips. This is exactly what had happened to him, he thought.

Sage continued, "Your soul doesn't want you to do things that you're already good at. Because that means stagnation. And so you start hating that job or that business after a while."

"Yes."

"See. Your real Purpose, your greatest service to the world is something that you actually *don't* want to do."

"No, that's not right! I *do* want to do it."

"Yes and no. Part of you does. But another part of you will do anything to prevent it from happening. The ego part."

"WHY?"

"Because it would mean the death of the current ego. It will require you to become a different self, with a new system of values and a way of seeing the world. Your current ego is afraid of that. It wants to protect itself – so it will fight to keep things as they are. It's very hard to win that battle without a good mentor by your side… this is one of the reasons why most people don't succeed. They don't know about that secret enemy that's holding them back."

Mike frowned. "I see."

"And here's another aspect of this. Your ego doesn't believe you can make it happen. Because your greatest service, your true mission in life is way outside of your comfort zone. And so it appears too grand, too inaccessible to even try to go for it."

"That definitely makes sense…"

"Discovering your Purpose is a Hero's Journey, you see," Sage said. "And there's always a refusal of the call before the actual magic starts to happen."

Mike smiled at the mention of one of his favourite books. "I know about the Hero's Journey," he said. "But doesn't the refusal happen before meeting a mentor?"

"Not in this case," Sage replied. "At the beginning, most people think they want to start their quest. They get excited to start. But once they realise what it involves, some of them turn around."

"Can someone really turn around?"

"Not truly, no. If one refuses to go forward, he often starts on a downward spiral. Or he's forced to retrace his steps at a later date. But you can never go back to what you once were."

"Hmm."

Sage threw him a magician's smile. "Tempted to change your mind?"

Mike looked back seriously but with a hint of defiance in his eyes. "This is *not* going to happen." He said accentuating every word. "I'll show you. I'm not like everyone else."

Mike's homework notes:

"Learn the meditation warmup (the link is https://newerasuperhero.com/medi-warmup)"

"Try to get clarity on what my Why actually is…WHY do I want to change my life, deep down?"

"Look up other examples of horizontal development in nature for reference."

THE SUPERHERO'S JOURNEY

CHAPTER 5: BECOMING A TORNADO

"Decide what kind of life you actually want. And then say no to everything that isn't that."
– Melanie Mackie

They met again in the same study, surrounded by the soothing whiteness of the walls. This time, Sage brought their coffees himself. He wore a white Prada top instead of his usual collared shirt. It was a hot day outside.

"There's something I wanted to ask," Mike said as soon as he sat down. "I kept thinking about it after our first meeting."

"Go ahead," Sage told him lightly.

Mike paused for a moment looking down then blurted out, "What's the deal with the lightsabers?!"

"What about them?" Sage smiled.

"Just… why?"

"They are to test if someone would be a good student,"

Sage said. "Once upon a time, I used metal swords, but they are cumbersome... and somewhat problematic for beginners. Lightsabers are easier. And also, way cooler. Especially after dark." Sage took a swallow of his coffee.

"That's for sure." Mike sniffed. "But...how does that— I mean, what kind of test is that?"

"It's simple. The way you handle a sword—or any weapon of that kind—shows not only the strength of your body and your mind but also how you deal with challenges. Your balance, your integrity, and your willingness to stand up for what you believe in. And also, whether or not you're easily swayed by fear."

"Wow! That's a lot. How do you know about that?"

"An old habit," Sage replied offhandedly. "From ancient China, most likely. Or maybe the Roman Empire...? Not sure. I've been handling swords for as long as I can remember."

Mike choked on his coffee. "What?! How long ago was that??"

Sage wrinkled his forehead. "About 2000 years ago. It doesn't really matter."

Mike gasped. "No, wait...! I need to know!"

"Not right away. It won't do much for you right now," Sage told him evenly. "There will be time to talk about it at a later stage. I told you I was older than you thought."

"You did..." Mike stared at his mentor in utter disbelief.

"Are you... immortal, then?!"

Sage chucked. "No. Just been around for a while." For a moment, his gaze seemed tired. "Anyway," he added. "Let's get back on track."

"Yes, of course," Mike said softly, his mind still blank with shock. "Let's. What's the agenda for today?"

"Some physics. You need to understand the centripetal and the centrifugal principle."

"I don't know what 'centripetal' means," Mike admitted.

"The word was coined by Isaac Newton," Sage said. "From the Latin *centrum* meaning "centre" and *petere* "to rush out". Simply speaking, it describes the movement from the outside towards the centre. It's like a water vortex in the sink after the cork is pulled out.

Its opposite is the centrifugal force whose name also originates in Latin. The second part here, fugere, means "to flee". Like 'veni, vidi, fugi'." Sage squinted one eye.

"I don't understand Latin," Mike shrugged.

"I came, I saw, I fled."

"Shouldn't it be 'I conquered'?" Mike asked doubtfully. "The famous saying by Julius Ceasar."

"For him, it was so. For others, results may vary." Sage said with irony in his voice. "So, these two forces move in opposite directions. A water vortex in the sink rotates inwards, while a tornado whirls outwards."

Mike rubbed the bridge of his nose. "Alright, and how does knowing that help me get closer to my Purpose?"

"By making you aware of your life dynamic," Sage told him. "Not understanding this is what keeps many people stuck."

"How so?"

"Think about what the word 'Purpose' actually entails. When you say that something is used according to its purpose, you mean that it's being used as intended – the way it's been designed to function."

"Yes."

"This is true for us human beings as well. You need to learn to function in the optimal way for you to feel that you live the way you were meant to. Which means, being centrifugal."

"Please explain."

"We are part of the universe, as you know. And the way the universe 'sees' us is simply as bundles of energy. Imagine everyone being a tiny lightbulb. Now, what's the purpose of a lightbulb?"

Mike pursed his lips. "To shine? To give light?"

"Precisely. Imagine if you got a lightbulb for your room but instead of lighting it up, it would suck in all the brightness instead. Bet you wouldn't be happy."

Mike snorted. "That would be a rubbish lightbulb for sure."

"Here's what it means for you, or anyone who wants to live their Purpose. We are supposed to share ourselves with the world. To give value, in whichever form it is relevant to us. To shine our light, so to speak. Then the rewards will come. Not just the financial and social rewards but also something greater – an in-depth sense of one's true value and one's place in the world. A heartfelt sense that you stand for something, that you truly matter."

Mike nodded, frantically scribbling away in his digital notepad.

"An Austrian philosopher called Alfred Alder," Sage continued, "maintained that our true sense of inner confidence and fulfilment comes from what he called 'a community feeling' or 'being of use to someone'. When you feel that you somehow made a difference in other people's lives. He even went as far as assuming that *that*, in and of itself, is our Purpose."

"But it's not?"

"It's not quite as simplistic. Having a positive impact on other people's lives is a great feeling for sure, but it's only one of the ways to get to your optimal life dynamic. It's one of its aspects. At its core, this dynamic is about expansion and presence."

"Expansion and presence?"

"Yes. As you know, the universe constantly expands – and being synchronous with the flow of life is generally a smart move. We human beings 'expand' through learning and conscious personal evolution. The more you grow mentally and spiritually, the more your level of energy grows, and so does your impact and your sense of contribution and fulfilment."

Mike ruffled his hair. He was wearing a cosy old blue t-shirt, with his company's logo partially faded in the wash. "Alright, I see how that works."

"If you stop in your self-development and stagnate," Sage continued, "you turn into a piece of rock in a river. The current of life always moves. And if it can't carry you along, you become like an obstacle it hits. You get cut off from the flow of life. That was one of the reasons for the pain you felt."

The analogy seemed simple and yet Mike struggled to connect it with his circumstances. He tossed the pen in his fingers and looked contemplatively through the window behind Sage.

"Powerlessness," Sage explained, noticing Mike's gaze. "The sense of being out of control and wasting your time."

"Ah! Yes, that rings the bell."

"If you go with the flow of life, you feel empowered and supported. Pumped. Excited. You move forward faster. The more you evolve, the more satisfaction and joy you will feel."

"So, just keep constantly learning new things?"

"Learning new things is a good habit and an interesting pastime for sure. But in itself, it only serves to entertain your ego mind. I'm talking about expanding your mind through inner transformation, inner alchemy. The caterpillar and the butterfly kind of journey."

Mike rubbed his chin. "I see."

"To live your Purpose, which is to live 'as designed', you need two things. First, to be aligned with the universal flow, the flow of time. And second, to be rooted in your polarity. That is why you need to be a tornado."

"I'm lost," Mike admitted. "What does that actually mean, in practical terms?"

"A man must act in alignment with his masculine core. It's what you need to do if you want to step into your true personal power, confidence and inner peace. Everything that throws you onto the opposite side of the spectrum weakens and hinders you. Not only on the personal level but also in your business. Often, it puts you into a depressed state as well."

"That suc— I mean, I don't like the idea of it." Mike crossed his arms. "So, what should I do, specifically?"

"We were just getting to that point," Sage told him patiently. "Do you know the difference between the feminine and the masculine?"

"Like, men and women?"

"No. The feminine and the masculine, Yin and Yang, the Lunar and the Solar dynamics, are universal principles. They find their expression everywhere, not only in humans. But the tools you have, like your physical body, prime you to benefit from one of them more. Make the masculine polarity your guiding star and you will keep winning.

Here's what the difference is. What we refer to as 'masculine' and 'feminine', from the universal point of view are simply the electric and the magnetic forces. The plus and the minus, push and pull.

Going back to the centrifugal and the centripetal movement, the centrifugal dynamic is masculine. It represents the expansion, the push. Its focus is 'from me – into the world.' You decide who you want to be, how you want to serve, what business you create – and you take it out there and share it with others. You are the source of that impact and other people are the recipients. It is you who decides and takes action."

"Can it be any other way?" Mike twisted his mouth contemplatively.

"Yes. Ever been on Reddit?" Sage smiled.

"Reddit?" Mike flashed his eyebrows. "Plenty of times."

"Ever seen posts like, 'What niche should I choose for my business to make money fast'?"

"Yes…" Mike answered, still baffled by the idea of a spiritual mentor using Reddit, "There are lots."

Sage cast him an ironic sidelong glance. "Not all teachers spend their lives on mountaintops," he said. "Improvise. Adapt. Overcome." He curved up a corner of his lips.

Mike snorted with surprise. *This man is really something else*, he thought.

"So," Sage continued. "People who post such questions are living in the centripetal state. Their key approach is, 'What's in it for me?' They don't create new paths, they follow someone else's. Copy even. They want the energy to move from the outside towards them. Money is a form of energy, too. Their attitude is centred on what they can pull in from the world rather than what they can give it. That's the Yin or the Lunar dynamic."

"But doesn't everyone start a business to get something from the world? Like money?"

"Technically yes, we do. But the motivation is different. For the electric, Solar principle, the primary drive is to make a difference. To express oneself and touch people's lives in some way. Not to simply get a new yacht or a new house."

Mike nodded.

"When you seek to express yourself, you don't ask 'what niche is the most profitable?' because you know that nearly every niche can be, if tackled right. So instead, you strive to bring out the best product or service out there. You want to create a legacy, an impact. You blaze your own trail. You set a trend rather than follow a trend. That's the Yang, masculine way.

A real life example: if you create new cutting-edge technology, a new AI model, or a revolutionary marketing or coaching approach, you're acting in the Yang way. But if you find something that someone else has created, buy the patent or the course and then merely put your own branding on it, that's Yin, the Lunar way. Do you see the difference?"

"Yes."

"Here's a secret… if you follow the opposite polarity for long enough, it will start jarring on your soul. You'll start feeling low, fed up with yourself, and exasperated with your business. No amount of money can fix that."

Mike doodled a sad face in his notepad. "So what can fix it, then?" he asked.

"Aligning with your Purpose and polarity," Sage said. "Don't come from the place of 'what I can get' but rather, 'how can I be of the greatest service?' Sounds a bit lofty but it's very practical at its core. If you send your force – your gift, your passion, your best effort – out, what you want will then come to you. The universe will see to keep the balance. But if you try to pull things in towards you, there will be an opposite force pulling them away."

Mike played with the pen in his fingers. "I've heard people saying similar things before. I mean, in terms of service and passion. But I've also seen guys who've been putting in an honest effort for years and still couldn't get where they wanted to be."

"Most likely, they haven't been following their polarity fully," Sage replied. "Every person is different, of course. But in the case of those guys, they might have been going down the Yin path, following someone else's blueprint. That would create a conflict between their soul and their ego mind, which sabotaged their progress. It might have also been that they didn't dare to face the world."

"Hmm?"

"You'd be surprised how many people are forced into 'lives of quiet desperation' by their fear. You see, true impact and greatness require *presence*."

"Please go on."

"The presence I'm talking about is the willingness to take things as they come. The courage to be seen, to be in a spotlight. That light you give off as you serve draws people's eyes to you. They approach you with all sorts of intentions. They post snide comments on the internet and send you nasty emails. And so some people choose to hide. You know, they seem to be out there giving value, but from 'behind a screen'. An alias for the name, a pixelated robot head for the profile picture." Sage squinted his eyes in a knowing half-smile.

"What?" Mike breathed out. "How did you know I've got that on my profile pic?"

"I looked you up."

Mike looked down and rubbed his neck. "It's Grumbot," he said. "From Hermitcraft. Don't judge me. I used to play that." Mike looked discomfited like a kid who did something naughty. "I don't play these days anymore."

"Fair enough. But why are you using that picture instead of your own face?"

"I thought it was kind of cool and funny, I guess…" Mike caught Sage's shrewd stare directed at him. "Well… I—" he set his lips. "Fine! You win. You're right. I felt kind of awkward putting my face out there. We're a marketing company, not a modelling agency, who cares! I thought nobody would care what I look like, anyway."

"And how did it make you feel?"

Mike chewed his lip. "Safe, I guess? Kind of invisible. Both in the good and the bad sense. But when I think about it now…" He paused. "Kind of small, too. In a strange way. Like, in a way, I don't really matter."

"Hiding and evading is also the Lunar tactic. Can you see how such feelings would prevent you from stepping into your power and your greatest service? To succeed, you'd have to be present and seen. By many."

"Fair enough, that makes sense."

"Imagine a tornado being shy," Sage smiled lightly.

"Hah! No…that wouldn't happen. That's not how it works."

"Exactly. Now you know why you need to become a tornado."

"Where do I start?"

"You already have. Realisation is the first step. The other ones, we will discuss next time."

Mike's homework notes:

"Think about who I really want to be and what life I want to live."

"Have a look at where I step back when I should step forward in my decisions."

"Which parts of my business and my life are truly aligned, and which ones may be influenced by other people's ideas of 'how things should be done'?"

"Before making a decision or starting doing something, check if that decision or that action is making sense to me personally."

"Download the Instant Transcendence sound-only track for meditation (external link https://newerasuperhero.com/transcendence)"

THE SUPERHERO'S JOURNEY

CHAPTER 6:
THE CHOSEN ONE

"Do not act following customary beliefs."
- Miyamoto Musashi, The Way of Walking Alone

It didn't go the way Mike had planned.

His team reached out in the evening, at the start of the day in their time, to let him know that the big potential client they had lined up for so long had finally committed to working together. Great news. He wanted to meet at Mike's office the day after tomorrow, though. That meant a rushed journey back, and a long flight.

The flight part didn't bother him. He always took it as an opportunity to do some focused work. Being close to the sky seemed to enhance his thinking and creativity. At 35,000ft above the ground, problems and worries seemed different. Less daunting, somehow.

This time, Mike had *a lot* to think about.

As soon as the seatbelt lights went off, he reclined his seat and threw his hands behind his head. In his noise-blocking earphones, the engine buzzing turned into a soft hum. The sound curiously reminded him of the Transcendence meditation track he got from Sage. Listening to it made entering a meditative state a breeze. *Could that humming noise be the reason he could focus better when flying?*

Right now, that didn't matter though.

While one part of him was excited about finally signing up that long-chased client, the other part was annoyed that he didn't get to hear the end of the tornado story and expressing the masculine principle.

Mike bent down, rummaged in his bag and pulled out his notepad. He swiped through the pages to his most recent notes and read through them again. This all was getting crazy interesting.

He looked through the window, at the clouds majestically passing by.

How much of his life did he actually decide on, up until now?

It was *his* choice to start a business and escape the 9 to 5, sure. Why this model, this type of business, though? 'Because it was easy', a quiet voice in his head answered. 'Quick money. An easy-to-learn skill. Never run out of clients. People always need marketing.'

Mike chewed his lip. *Was it the kind of mark he wanted to leave on the world? The kind of legacy he'd like to create?* He wasn't sure. His business certainly helped other people. It also helped him get the life and the freedom that he wanted. And yet… something was off. *Why? Why did it start feeling like a drag?* Mike's lips curved in an ironic smile at the aviation analogy.

Ask Sage about the next steps, he wrote in his notepad and underlined the words.

He thought again about his unusual mentor. Sage was like nobody he's ever met. 'Not all teachers spend their lives on mountaintops,' a phrase said in passing floated through Mike's mind.

How does that guy remember what happened thousands of years ago?! Mike rubbed his face. There was something uncommon about being in Sage's presence. Mike realised that their sessions together made him feel different from before. More focused, more inspired. Kind of invincible, in a way he struggled to put into words. He would much rather be sitting in his study right now asking questions, than flying back.

Oh well. Mike was the type that put responsibilities first, fun second. His team relied on him to get that deal finalised.

The world back home was cool and grey with overcast. It felt a bit surreal; hazy and dream-like; probably due to jetlag.

Mike did what was expected of him, going through the familiar motions, saying the familiar things. They worked in the past, and they worked this time. But they also brought back the familiar feeling that 'everything sucked'. Even the signed contract, after a brief spike of joy, suddenly didn't matter.

That sure was disappointing. Mike expected to get a kick from achieving a goal that he'd been chasing for so long. But now, when it was a done deal, it simply wasn't important anymore. If anything, he felt a little tired.

Back in his apartment, Mike flopped on the sofa and pulled his phone out. It was late but he didn't feel like sleeping.

He stared for a few minutes at the open window of his Telegram app, hesitating to send a message at this hour. Then he remembered about the time zone difference. Cheered up by the thought, Mike found Sage amongst his contacts and typed up a message. He re-read it, winced, and deleted it without sending, though. He typed another one but then deleted it, too.

He suddenly had a weird feeling as though Sage was with him in the room, watching his failing attempts with a smile. Mike shook his head. 'Damn jetlag…'

He looked outside, at the darkness dotted with lit-up windows, then typed simply, "Hello, do you know what to do when everything sucks? Thank you in advance." and pressed 'send'.

"That's good news," came an enigmatic answer. "Become mindful of what exactly you feel."

"I *don't want* to feel that. And how can it be good news?!"

"It means that you're getting ready to begin your *real* life. Your current reality is too small for you."

My current reality is too small for me, Mike repeated to himself with a hint of frustration. His tired brain was slow to make sense of that. Still, it rang true, somehow.

"Alright, and what do I do about it?" He realised it might have come across as too brash and added, "Please."

"It's not easy but you can do it," Sage replied. "You'll have to accept your role in your unfolding destiny, and the destiny of the world."

'What does that even—? Argh. Note to self, talking about deep concepts at 2 am was a stupid idea,' Mike thought. He rubbed his temples trying to focus. "What do you mean? What role?" He typed.

"You won't like it."

"I don't like it already. Bring it on."

"You'd have to accept being the Chosen One."

Oh, f-ck that…! Mike's sleep-deprived brain had finally given up. That's it. He'd gone crazy. Or Sage had gone crazy. Or both.

"Nope. That's nuts."

"I told you you wouldn't like it. But that's the only way," Sage said unruffled. "Now, try to get some sleep."

THE SUPERHERO'S JOURNEY

CHAPTER 7: ACTING 'BECAUSE', NOT 'BECAUSE OF'

"I don't buy into some stupid fantasy like that," Mike said to himself angrily in the morning, slobbering shaving cream on his face. He twisted his wrist awkwardly when putting the bottle back and the foam spray hit the mirror, spattering everywhere. "F-ck!"

Sage's words from last night left him unsettled and unexpectedly irked. Specifically, Mike was annoyed with the part of his mind that got giddily excited at the prospect of becoming a Chosen One. That little part of him that always dreamt of hearing those words, ever since he was a kid. That part that never stopped hoping.

"Shut up! You're not some dumb kid," he told himself sternly while energetically cleaning the mirror with a towel. "You can't believe some glorified BS, no matter who says it. I bet it's some weird marketing trick." He threw the towel in the sink and walked out of the bathroom.

As the day went on, Mike's annoyance grew bigger. 'He can't be serious. Surely. What crap is that? How is this going to help me find my Purpose? He should have given me a diagram or a questionnaire to fill out... About my skills and what I like and such. To help me figure out what I should do. Not some weird stupid unrelated twaddle! That's it. I've had enough. I'm going to write to that dude and say I'm cancelling my training,' something in him shrivelled at that thought but Mike was adamant. He opened his email client and started typing.

It was then that his phone rang. It was Luke, the very guy who had talked him into this damn nonsense in the bar that night. Mike set his lips but after a moment's hesitation pressed 'accept'.

"What?" he asked brusquely.

"How is it going?" Luke asked upbeat, ignoring Mike's tone.

"It's *not* going," Mike grunted. "You better stick to your crypto data stuff because your life advice sucks."

"What? Can't be that bad. What happened?"

"Don't wanna talk about it."

"Oh, come on."

"That dude is weird! He is— He just gets on my nerves! The stuff he says... Can't be legit. I'm cancelling with him."

Luke laughed. "Sounds like he pushed you out of your comfort zone? And so what? One push and you're out, like a f-king douche?" He laughed again. "Being uncomfortable is how you grow, bro."

"Shut up!!" Mike growled at him. "Go be f-king smug

somewhere else. Bro."

"No, listen," Luke's voice sounded serious now. "Sage is good. He's the best out there. If anyone can guide you to where you want to be, it's him."

"What makes you say that?"

Luke paused. "I know about him a bit. I've heard stories … from some mutual friends."

"You know a bit?" Mike didn't care to hide the mockery in his voice.

"Uhm…" Luke suddenly sounded almost diffident. "I'm a bit envious, you know."

"Envious of what?" Mike blinked, dumbfounded.

"That you got to train with him. That you got accepted. One day… maybe one day I'll try as well."

"What…? I thought you trained with him?"

"No," Luke said in an awkward tone of voice. "But I wish I could. I just—"

"You just what?"

"I guess I don't have the guts to do it yet," Luke admitted reluctantly. "I heard that it's tough. I dunno if I'd even get accepted. Maybe one day. Don't share that on social! Don't tell anyone I said that."

"Get off! And who is the douche here, huh?!"

"Err, whatever. I did say that one day I would! So there."

"Hmm…" The anger that Mike carried all day had gradually evaporated. In its place, some other feeling had sprung up, strong and clear, yet he couldn't find the name for it. "Well, fine. OK. I'll give it another shot."

"Let me know how it goes?" Luke asked eagerly.

"Will do," Mike rubbed his nose. "What was it that you heard about him, by the way?"

"I heard… that he can make strange things happen. He has some abilities. You probably won't believe me anyway. Maybe it's best if you ask him yourself."

"After the lightsabers, I'll believe anything, I guess," Mike huffed.

"Lightsabers…? What lightsabers?" Luke sounded flummoxed.

"A story for another time," Mike told him tiredly. "I'm falling asleep as I talk. F-king hate jetlag."

"Fair enough. No probs, chat later."

Mike put his phone on the desk, leant back in his chair and closed his eyes. It was only 3 pm but his body still believed it was close to midnight.

He dozed off before he knew it.

In his dream, he saw a white hall with two streams that ran through it: one flowed tinkling towards Mike, and the other one away from him. A tall person dressed in white and with a golden mask came forth from within the hall. He asked Mike to choose the stream to step into.

Mike pointed at the one flowing away from him. "That one."

"Very good," the figure said in Sage's voice. He took off his mask and Mike realised it was, indeed, Sage. "The other one would kill you."

"What kind of test was that?!"

"You choose to live either rooted in your future or your past. If you turn to the past, it will consume you until nothing is left."

"And the future?"

"It will challenge you, but it'll build you up. Remember, everything you do should be 'because', not 'because of'."

"I don't understand," Mike said, stepping into the coolness of the stream.

"Go for what you *want*, not what you want to avoid. If you're rooted in your past, you'll tend to make decisions based on the fears or traumas from that past. You'll repeat it endlessly. You'll act *because of*. But if your choices are future-driven, you'll act *because* you want to achieve something. Because it makes sense to your future self."

More people drew in from all sides and gathered around, listening. "Look!" One of them said pointing at Mike, "The Chosen One."

"What? No!" Mike turned sharply to him. "Stop it!"

But it was too late. "The Chosen One... The Chosen

One…" rolled through the crowd.

Mike looked at Sage helplessly. "Please tell them to stop," he pleaded. "It's weird. I don't want it!"

"What do you want, then?"

"I don't know… some quiet normal life," Mike said uncertainly.

"That's not true." Sage's eyes directed straight at him were the colour of deep gold. "And you know it."

Mike sighed and dropped his head. "Yes, you're right. I do." He watched the water running around his feet. "But that other role… I don't like it, either. It seems too grand. And wacky. More like a fantasy. I don't believe it's true."

"If it *were* true, would you want it then?"

Mike took a deep breath. That part of him he'd been trying to stifle and fight off, had finally won. "Yes," he admitted simply then lifted his head and smiled a broad smile. Suddenly, he felt free. "I would. I always felt… something like this. But it's a fantasy, though."

"This world is a strange place," Sage told him. "Trust who you're becoming."

Mike opened his eyes to the buzzing and blinking of his phone reminder. It was exactly 4.30 pm and a good half an hour until his next Zoom call. He grabbed his notepad and started scribbling frantically before the memory of his dream faded away.

CHAPTER 8: A DEEP DIVE: BEHIND THE VEIL

"The key to growth is the introduction of higher dimensions of consciousness into our awareness."
- Lao Tzu

Only a week later, Mike was back in the all-white study, where Sage with his enigmatic smile and his statutory cup of coffee waited for him.

It felt good to be back.

"I have a question," Mike announced immediately after the greeting part was over. "Two questions, actually."

"Start with the second one," Sage told him.

Mike flashed his eyebrows. "Alright." But then he realised that Sage had an uncanny way of knowing things in advance. "I want to understand that idea you spoke about earlier. It doesn't sit right with me."

"The Chosen One?"

"Yes."

"Ah, that's pretty straightforward," Sage smiled lightly. "It's simply a shift in perspective. Here's how it works… Let's start from the personal level. To succeed in bringing change, meaning, and value, you have to be the hero, the protagonist of your own story. In other words, become the centre of power in your world."

"The centre of power?"

"Imagine yourself like a sun surrounded by planets. Those planets are your circumstances, events, and other people in your life. You are the one that decides which ones stay in your life, how much of your energy and time goes to each one, and so on. But also, it is *you* who pulls them forth out of the sea of possibilities in the first place. You can say that you manifest them from the quantum field."

"Alright…"

"This is not an egoic concept. Assuming the position of 'the one who decides' empowers you and puts things into the right perspective. It naturally creates the mindset that makes things happen. In other words, it helps you 'become a tornado'. You realise that you're responsible for your life experience, and also for what you share with others. So this is one part of it."

"And the other part?" Mike asked without lifting his gaze

from his notepad.

"The other part is universal. We don't live in a vacuum. Our existence is invisibly yet intricately linked with other people and things that share this world with us. We affect them, without even knowing. And the more power we have, the greater that influence is."

"What do you mean? What kind of power?"

"Ready for a deep dive?" Sage squinted at him somewhat elvishly.

"Always."

"You know that you're not just your physical body?"

"I heard about it, yes. There was a CIA research project from the 1980s that explained that we are, basically, holographic fields that interact with other holographic fields. Just energy vibrating at different speeds."

Sage nodded. "The universe 'sees' us as bundles of energy, scattered fragments of the universal hologram. Each of us not only witnesses, but is also called to co-create in the evolution of the world. Now we're getting close to what your Purpose actually is."

Mike responded with a curious smile. "You have my full attention," he said.

"I know you're frustrated that I didn't give you forms and diagrams to complete," Sage said ironically, "But there's a reason for that."

Mike snorted. 'How did he figure it out?' he wondered.

"You're not the first one to deal with such doubts," Sage responded to his thoughts. "It's a common theme—"

"You can read my thoughts, you really can!" Mike burst out. "Admit it."

"Hmm, no. I'm just perceptive," Sage said with a smile that made it impossible to tell whether he was serious or not. "Anyway, the reason why I don't start with diagrams is because it would be pointless."

"Pointless…? Why? Every other purpose coach—"

"I'm not a coach," Sage corrected him evenly. "And I'm not every other, either."

"Who are you, then?"

"You call people like me 'removers of ignorance'," Sage replied with a note of pensiveness. "But I don't like that word. 'Mentor' would be adequate. I'm a researcher and a teacher… and an adventurer, I guess. Also, a geek." He smirked.

"What?" Mike's eyebrows went up.

"*Anyway*," Sage continued with more emphasis, "let's get back on track. Diagrams and questionnaires are pointless to start with, for two reasons. Firstly, your Purpose is not what you *do*, but who you *are*. Or more accurately, who you're *becoming*. Do you understand the difference?"

"I think so," Mike answered uncertainly.

"It is 'who' that comes first, not 'what'. Who you are, and

how you see yourself, dictates what you can and cannot do. And even what you do and don't allow yourself to think and dream about. It also influences what you focus on in life. Is it clearer now?"

"Yes."

"Good. So to live your Purpose, you need to first become the version of yourself who can do it. In other words, you need to grow spiritually, mentally and emotionally until you reach the level at which you can operate in optimal alignment."

Mike nodded and Sage continued, "That new upgraded version of you will think and act differently from the current you. He will have different likes, passions and priorities. You can't yet see them from where you currently are. And so if I gave you a questionnaire, it would simply reflect your past not your future. All the answers would be wrong. So that's the other reason."

"That reminds me of a dream I had a few days ago," Mike said.

"About the two streams," Sage filled in the details for him.

"Y-yes… What?! How did you know?" Mike gaped at Sage.

"I was there," Sage said simply. "It was me talking to you back then."

"HOW?! This is insane…"

"I teach my students in dreams every now and then. Sometimes, it's easier to talk that way. You'll learn that too, in time."

Mike bit his lip, suddenly remembering what Luke had said about the 'strange skills' Sage had.

"Sure…ok…" He muttered trying to gather thoughts.

"This world is a strange place, I told you," Sage said mildly. "You'll get used to it. Being a superhero comes at a cost. But paying the price for growth is infinitely better than suffocating in a reality that's too small for you." He directed his warm knowing stare at Mike. "Your Purpose is not a career choice. Trust me, if you simply start a new business keeping your current perspective of the world, before long, you'd feel as stifled by this new venture as you are now. This is a trap some people fall into. They get a new job or start a new business every time they feel like their reality is closing in on them. At first, the newness is exciting. But it soon wears out. What remains are disappointment and burnout. Then their life just passes by."

"Vertical vs horizontal development," Mike said, proud that he remembered his notes.

"Exactly."

"Your soul doesn't want to do again things that it's already learnt. It doesn't want you to do things you're 'good at'. The restlessness and anxiety you feel is a call for growth. When everything sucks, it means that you're called to start your Great Adventure, to transform yourself and the world around you."

"Sounds grand."

"And here we come again to the second part of being the 'Chosen One'," Sage said. "Your individual consciousness is a fragment of the universal hologram. A spark from the universal consciousness. There's an immeasurable number of such fragments, but they differ in size. The bigger they are, the more influence they have on the world around them. You can imagine it like the celestial bodies in the universe - the greater their mass, the stronger their gravitational pull. Except *we* push energy *out* instead. A bit like white holes."

"I see."

"That's not all. The more energy someone has at their command, the more the universe 'notices' them. And while everyone's thoughts and choices matter, those people's thoughts and choices matter more. This is because they have a greater power to bend and shift reality. They are trendsetters and the changers of history. You can see them as 'spiritual special forces'. They are the Chosen Ones from the universe's standpoint. "

"Where are you heading with this?"

"You're one of those people."

"Hmm?"

"As a soul goes through its lifetimes, it gradually remembers who he or she is. But even as the soul is getting that clarity, the conscious mind may still have no idea. Part of your training will be to align the two so they see eye to eye. You'll then understand fully what I mean, which will make things a lot easier.

For now, just accept this as a working theory: your soul is old enough to become dissatisfied with a plain mundane life. It wants more. This is where that internal pressure and anxiety you feel stem from."

Mike frowned and rubbed the bridge of his nose. "I… do feel it," he admitted. "It's hard to put into words. The 'you should be doing more, greater things' kind of feeling. It stresses me out in a way. Because I don't even know what that 'more' may be. But it keeps haunting me. It's annoying."

"What did you do about it?"

"What was I supposed to do? I don't even know…! Whatever I did, it didn't work. All that self-development stuff." Mike said with a tone of exasperation. "That's why I'm here…You said that my soul wants more. What does it want?"

"It wants you to start living as yourself, first of all."

Mike blinked, confused. "What? I AM living as myself!"

"No," Sage told him mildly but matter-of-factly. "As it stands, you don't even know what being yourself feels like."

"What do you mean?! I am here, right now, being myself."

"No," Sage repeated with a hint of a smile. "But you're on your way there. Keep going."

CHAPTER 9: THE COURAGE TO BE YOURSELF

*"First say to yourself what you would be,
and then do what you have to do."*
- Epictetus

Mike was pleased with himself. He found a great gym only a short walk away, which meant he could get back to his morning workouts. As far as he was concerned, it was the best way to start the day.

Female gymgoers in their skin-tight outfits were usually a bonus, but today his mind was occupied with something else. He didn't even look around, just went straight to the weights rack, picked up the weights and looked at himself in the mirror.

While working out, he reflectively studied his body and his face as though he saw them for the first time.

"You don't know what being yourself feels like." Sage's words from yesterday rang in his mind. *What did he mean, I don't know?!* Mike studied his reflection again. His arms certainly looked good. He smirked.

"You're not living as your true self," Sage told him before they parted yesterday. "Your life doesn't reflect your true priorities, or even what you actually love. That's why it feels like going through the motions…because it is. You're showing the world a mask instead of your real face."

Mike twisted his lips remembering the conversation. He didn't like what he heard and yet he couldn't deny that it made sense. His life was…comfortable, and that's it. It wasn't inspiring, and it wasn't fulfilling. And the stupid feeling that he was meant for something more, which haunted him for years – and at which Sage masterfully poked – was still there, annoying him.

Mike sighed, put the weights down and picked up his water bottle. It tasted sour and funny from the electrolytes, but he got used to that taste over time. He hardly noticed it now.

He realised he was looking forward to today's meeting with Sage. His mind was buzzing with questions.

At the appointed time, he was at the familiar door, clutching a bag with his notepad.

Sage opened the door himself, with a takeaway cup of coffee in his hand. "Hello there," he smiled. He wore his usual grey jeans and a white shirt with the sleeves rolled up.

Upstairs, Mike customarily plopped on the sofa and started pulling his writing utensils out of his bag. Sage stood by the window looking outside.

"Did you know," he said out of the blue, sipping his coffee, "that in Japanese, the character for the 'sky' also means 'emptiness'..." He paused and looked up. "Emptiness with the stars beyond. The stars are always there...but we can't see them because we're blinded by the closeness of just one. Which is not even the biggest or the brightest. Our lives are like that." His face turned pensive. "We forget our true priorities because we're blinded by the shiny object syndrome. By what's right there, in front of us, even if that something is not the best thing. But it's close...and distracting. Businesses, relationships." He paused again. "Here, take your coffee," Sage finally turned to Mike offering him the other takeaway cup he picked up from the table. "Coffee is the best drink. Dark like intergalactic space." He smiled but his look remained distant.

"Are you alright?" Mike asked picking up on some strange melancholy in Sage's voice.

"Me? Yes, I'm fine. I just miss my old days sometimes."

Mike could swear Sage's eyes shimmered gold when he said that. *What?!* He nearly jerked up from his seat. *Who is this dude..?!* He suddenly felt apprehensive, almost scared.

Sage gave him one of those penetrating gazes of his and a corner of his lips twitched up. "Something's wrong?"

"Yes! Your eyes...!" Mike blurted out. "They—!!"

Sage snorted and took a swallow of his coffee. "Good advancements," his voice sounded content.

Mike gaped at him, too lost for words.

"This world is a stranger place than you might have realised up until now," Sage told him. "And as you learn to live as you truly are, you'll get to see the world as it is as well. It's a wild ride to begin with. But then you get used to it."

"Are you…even human…?" Mike winced as he heard himself asking that, almost as though his mouth moved by itself and the words simply rolled out, awkward and cringy. He rubbed his neck uncomfortably.

Sage threw him an ironic glance. "I guess you can say that…from a certain point of view."

"What?!"

"'Human' is a fuzzy term," Sage said. "If you mean 'human' as opposed to an alien or a ghost, then I'd qualify. If you mean it as a 'normie' who is sleepwalking through his life and lives below his true potential, then I'm not that."

Mike blinked trying to make sense of it all.

"You see, living as your true self involves ditching your limitations," Sage continued. "And underneath those self-imposed limitations, you're a divine being. I mean it literally. Seeing energy, distant healing, reading thoughts and such… it all comes with it. 'Humans' call such abilities superpowers. But they are simply an extension of our true nature."

Mike breathed out slowly through his pursed lips. "Superpowers…?" He tried to play it cool but his eyes sparked with excitement. "No way. OK, I want that."

Sage smiled. "You have them. It's only a matter of practice. See, no human would notice what you have."

"Notice what?"

"My eyes."

"Ah…yes. They—"

"—you'll get used to it," Sage assured him.

Mike leant back on the sofa and stared at the ceiling, thoughts rushing through his head. 'Who is this dude… No way, superpowers! I want that. No way…' He angled his neck to meet Sage's gaze. "So… I'm going to become someone like you?" he asked.

"Not quite like me. You'll become a superhero version of *yourself*. But yes, we'll share some similarities."

Mike went back to contemplating the ceiling. 'This surely can't be real… It's insane." He suddenly jerked upright. "So that guy, Taylor—"

"Tanner."

"Yes, him. That thing he did to the coffee. I saw that! I just didn't say anything."

"I know."

"Right," Mike rubbed his forehead. "So, let me get this

straight. You're telling me that I'm in a secret superhero HQ, and the only way for me to feel fulfilled and live my Purpose is to… to—he snorted—join the Avengers?" He studied Sage with open disbelief. "Come on, this can't be real."

"Well, that's not exactly what I said," Sage replied unruffled, "but roughly, yes. Stepping into your divine power is the only way that you can be your true self. Everything else would be an undershoot."

Mike hid his face in his hands. To an observer, it might seem like a sign of distress, but in reality, he did it only to hide his grin. Finally, he lifted his head and looked Sage square in the eye. "You have no idea how much I'm on board with this," he said.

"Good," Sage nodded casually, as though it was the answer he expected.

"You knew I'd say that?"

"I wouldn't be talking to you otherwise."

It was at that moment that Mike realised that Luke was right about things, on so many levels. He let out a long breath.

"So, I guess I should keep it a secret? My work here, I mean."

"It's not a secret per se, but I'd keep it under wraps," Sage said. "It's like building a business. Don't talk about the work that you do, not all people are supportive. Show them the results."

"Makes sense." Mike turned his stylus pen in his fingers. "But I kinda wish I could have someone to share this with. Even for accountability and such."

"Share it with other students in the group," Sage suggested.

"In the group?"

"Yes. I've got a mastermind group for my students. Now that you understand the basics, you can join in the discussion. I'll send you an invitation today. You'll meet some amazing people there."

Mike squinted smugly. "Does it mean that I've levelled up? Am I an initiate now?"

"That's correct."

"Nice," Mike squinted smugly imagining all the fun he'd have with superpowers. "By the way… I've got a friend who wants to train with you. It was him who recommended you in the first place."

"That's nice," Sage responded evenly. "But he's not ready yet."

Mike flashed his eyebrows. "Why?"

"Because he doesn't yet have what it takes. Challenge him to a lightsaber duel one day, and you'll see."

"What do you mean? What doesn't he have?"

"Courage," Sage said. "Becoming your true self takes a lot of courage."

"How do you know he doesn't have it?"

"Otherwise, he'd show up," Sage replied with half a smile.

'I don't have the guts to do it,' Luke's words floated in Mike's memory. "Hmm, I guess you're right."

"Just like not everyone becomes an entrepreneur, not everyone is ready to step into their Purpose in this lifetime. Sometimes it takes a while. Remember how you had to push through other people's disbelief and discouragement, and do it anyway?"

"Yes."

"Growing into your Purpose follows along similar lines. You're going to disturb the status quo. You're going to stop being the person you once were. Not everyone is going to like that. That's why I said what I said at the beginning. To step into your new life, you have to leave your old one behind."

"I think I understand it now. I couldn't make sense of it at the time," Mike admitted.

"Once you get there, it's a lot of fun. You'll likely look back at it as the best decision in your life. But the journey itself is not an easy one. If it were easy, everyone would be doing it. You'd have to face some serious fear and doubt, and keep moving forward, regardless."

"I've done that with my business, I can do it again," Mike told him firmly.

"Yes. That's why you will succeed. This time it's going to be harder, though… because the pushback will be from your own mind. It's trickier to shut it down than anything external that may come at you."

Mike set his lips. "I know. I've experienced it already."

"But you've won."

"Yes. Well, just about…but yes."

"The good news is that each such victory will make the next one easier. Do you know what started the internal conflict back then?"

"I… I just couldn't get my head around what you said," Mike twisted his mouth. "It was just… way out there. And I got angry."

"Why?"

"Because," Mike looked away, "I actually wanted it. Part of me did for sure. But then the other part said it was BS, and it sounded a lot more logical to think it was BS. I guess I was angry that I had to deal with that."

"That part of you that said it was BS, when you aligned with it, how did it make you feel?"

"I don't know… I felt bad," Mike paused searching for words. "Kind of small. That's it. I remember it made me kind of shrink inside. Like I betrayed something or someone. A nasty feeling."

"Remember it," Sage said.

Mike winced. "Why…?"

"For navigation. It will make it easier for you to map your way forward. That feeling you had, is the kind of life you get when listening to your fear. Small, lacking in confidence, suffocating. Filled with a sense of self-betrayal because fear kept making you step back when you needed to step forward. That's not your true self speaking. That's your ego-mask the part of you that doesn't want anything to change. It wants to remain cosy and accepted. To be validated by the people around you. The status quo lover."

"Screw the status quo!"

"With you on that," Sage nodded. "But you need courage to shake off that yoke. To step into the unknown. To stand for what you believe in, regardless of what others say. And to keep going until you see results."

"Got it." Mike picked up his coffee. It'd gone cold by then, but he finished it anyway. "That's definitely unlike any self-development training that I've done. Last question… How do I keep that courage going? It got pretty tough at one point. Like I thought I didn't want to do it anymore." Mike remembered his open email window with the Sage's address in it. "I want to have a better footing."

"You'll need a couple of mental anchors for that. The non-negotiables that will help you generate *lift*," Sage's eyes harboured a knowing smile.

"Oh yeah?" Mike squinted elvishly, appreciating the aviation analogy. "And what are they?"

"Come tomorrow. We'll talk about how planes fly."

Mike's homework notes:

"Fear is a sneaky enemy. It makes you live other people's definition of success and follow the status quo. This is not a way to live for a man. I need to create a list of my non-negotiables. What matters to me most?"

"All anger I feel is ultimately anger with myself, deep down."

"Like in business, keep going until you see the results."

CHAPTER 10: HOW PLANES FLY: THE 4 FORCES OF FLIGHT IN SELF-DEVELOPMENT

"Your whole idea about yourself is borrowed - borrowed from those who have no idea of who they are themselves."
- Osho

"It's good that you're always on time," Sage greeted Mike as soon as he stepped through the door. He wore all white except his overshirt with rolled up sleeves that was bright orange. "Our car should be here any minute now."

"Our car…?" Mike asked baffled.

"Yes. We're going on an adventure." Sage slung his phone

into his jeans pocket and turned to Mike with a broad yet somewhat elvish smile.

"Hmm…sure," Mike muttered uncertainly but then squinted with curiosity. "Why? Where?"

"You'll see," Sage answered casually, putting his aviator sunglasses on. "You need a change of perspective."

A white Tesla soundlessly rolled into the view, just then.

"That's us," Sage announced walking sprightly towards the gate. As he approached, the car's back doors lifted up like a pair of wings; the sunshine gleamed on the windows. Still perplexed, Mike followed his mentor and plunked on the seat next to him.

The doors went down with a soft clicking sound. The air-conditioned coolness felt great after the humid heat outside.

Mike threw his hands behind his head and turned to Sage questioningly. "Alright, now what?"

Sage glanced at his phone then nodded. "Patience," he said.

After an unexpectedly short ride through the maze of glass towers shrouded in mist, the taxi dropped them off at a helicopter landing area.

"Huh? Helicopters…?" Mike's eyebrows went up.

"Jets are no good for short distances," Sage threw him a magician's smile.

Mike grinned, drinking in the view of the helipads and the glossy sides of colourful whirlybirds waiting for their turn to take on the sky. "Neat," he said appreciatively pulling his sunglasses out of his pocket.

"We won't be able to talk once we're up, but I want you to be mindful of what you see and what you feel while there," Sage told him. "It will be useful for later."

"Got it."

Flying was great.

Flying was always great. Mike dutifully turned his gaze to the city of glass that stretched underneath. It was pretty but strangely alien at the same time. Perhaps 'utopian' would be the word. It looked more like a mirage than a real place, Mike thought, not for the first time. The lazy ocean beside it sparkled with sun glitter.

Mike wondered how it made him feel.

Excited for sure.

But what else?

He thought some more, trying to put into words a curious feeling that was growing in him. He realised it was the sense of freedom mixed with a tinge of something else… Uncertainty? Anxiety? There was a little bit of fear for sure.

Mike twisted his lips. Now that he reflected on it, the whole idea of throwing away everything he'd ever known for a vague hope of some uncertain freedom and fulfilment – some blurry visions that he couldn't even put into words – that whole idea started to look ludicrous.

He leant back and closed his eyes behind his sunglasses, idly tuning into the dull roar of the rotors. 'Don't listen to your fear,' he suddenly heard Sage's voice in his mind, as clear as though he was actually talking to him.

Mike angled his head and glanced at his mentor who sat beside him, looking through the window at something far in the distance.

'Fear, huh?' He closed his eyes again and focused on the thought. 'If you're not where you want to be in life, it's because you're living from the place of fear', a quote from long ago swam up at him. It rang annoyingly true. 'Fine,' Mike said mentally to that pesky inner voice. 'So you want to say that I live in fear, yeah?'

'Pretty much,' the inner voice replied insolently. 'Look how you throw a hissy fit each time you're even slightly challenged to expand your comfort zone. Loser.'

'Shut up!' Mike told it angrily. 'I've got a successful business. And a cool life. And look, I'm here right now, in a damned helicopter, miles from home! Doing something new. Listening to that dude...'

'And?' the voice teased him.

'What do you mean, 'and'?'

'Are you willing to even take in what he says?'

'What do you mean?'

'He keeps saying you'll have to become someone else…to live that awesome life that you want. And you don't even know what it's going to be like. Scary, no?'

Mike winced. 'Stop being a jerk. I can do it. I will.'

'Yeah…'

'F-king watch me.'

Mike snorted with annoyance and squashed the internal dialogue. He thought of the other possibility, of leaving everything as it was. Just going through the motions. A dull life with no way out.

His training was unusual for sure, but at least it gave him the long-searched sense of hope and freedom, and a feeling that he was doing something right. It felt as though his soul just wanted to go in that direction even though he struggled to explain his destination in words.

'As you start to walk on the way, the way appears,' another quote popped into his mind. *Who said that? Rumi…? Yeah, probably.* Mike felt calmer now, but also strangely pensive.

His thoughts wandered into the past. He wondered how many of his life turns and decisions were influenced by the sneaky enemy within – his own fear that told him to step back when he should have stepped forward. The fear that forced him to say 'yes' when he should have said 'no', and vice versa.

There were a few, for sure. But compared to other people he knew, he was still doing pretty well, Mike thought. He wouldn't have gotten to where he was in life if that wasn't the case. His lips curved up in a content half-smile.

But then… He also knew that he had stagnated for a while.

His self-development and his income have plateaued as though he had hit some invisible 'force field' ceiling, and he couldn't push through it. He hated to admit it, but on some days it made him feel seriously low.

And now, at long last, it finally looked like things were about to change.

Mike frowned. He was not going to allow any stupid fear to get in his way. He would grab this opportunity with both hands, and at least check where it might lead him.

Before he'd managed to finish that thought, they had landed.

On the way back, Mike kept silent, still ruminating over the things that had stirred up. Sage didn't talk either; and yet the silence was serene and warm, not awkward as it would have likely been with someone else.

They returned to the white chairs in Sage's study.

"What did you notice?" Sage finally broke the silence.

"Lots of stuff," Mike replied evasively.

"Including the stuff that weighs you down?" Sage asked again with a shrewd smile.

"What? Ah...yes, I guess," Mike said uncomfortably, avoiding looking Sage in the eye. "Some of it, too."

"You'll get a lot of clarity on your journey, and move forward much faster once you understand the four forces of flight...in self-development," Sage said handing Mike a piece of paper. "Have a look. It's pretty simple, really."

4 Forces of Flight in Personal Development

Earn more while doing what brings you fulfillment

LIFT
mentor
accountability
tribe
faith
values

DRAG
ego
(personal story)
traumas
fears
people's
opinion

THRUST
desire for
power and freedom
money
impact
Purpose
||
self-realization

WEIGHT
duties
routines
habits
life circumstances

"See here, on the left, you have what creates your drag."

"Uhm..."

"If you're not careful, these things will keep you stagnating in life. Things like fears, inner limitations, listening to the naysayers and trying to fit in. We tend to be more affected by this when we're younger but age is no guarantee of freedom. In other words, to make those drag forces lessen their grip, you have to make a conscious effort.

Just like a plane's aerodynamics can be improved to reduce drag, you can master your mind to achieve the same. And also, a physical plane wouldn't be able to fly if the force that pulls it back is stronger than the thrust that propels it forward."

"Well, of course!"

"See then, this is what happens in your life as well. If your fears and your desire to keep the status quo are stronger than your urge for personal growth and freedom, you'll stagnate, or even become less than you currently are. Your business would reflect that, too. Because true growth means breaking out and away from your old form, and becoming someone new."

"Gotcha."

"Another aspect is your personal story – the idea you have of yourself. What kind of person you are, what strengths and weaknesses you have, what you stand for, what you believe you can and cannot do."

"What if it's a good personal story, though?"

"For the majority of people, it isn't. What they have is usually a random mix based on the opinions of their parents, teachers, friends, coworkers, and past events. Almost nobody out there has a concept of self that actually reflects who they are."

"Interesting. But that story can be changed, right?"

"Yes. And this is one of the most important steps you'll need to take. You have to consciously create your new personal story, a new concept of self. Design it right, and you'll minimise the pushback forces that are keeping you stuck. Instead of being one of the elements of drag, it can contribute to your thrust – as it should be. With the right personal concept, you can finally allow yourself to be who you've always felt deep down, and more… and live an exciting life that reflects that truth. It's going to be your future homework."

"What, to live an exciting life?" Mike smirked.

"That too, but later," Sage answered with a glint of a smile in his eye. "First, you must craft the new concept of self."

"Great, I'll do that."

"Eventually, you will. Towards the end of our training. People like you typically can't complete this assignment straight away."

"Why not?"

"Their egos are too stubborn," Sage replied. His eyes seemed to look straight into Mike's soul.

"Oh yeah?" Mike said obstreperously. "Well, I don't care what limiting beliefs other people may have. I'm pretty sure *I* can do it. Just teach me how."

"Sure, if you're up for a little challenge, go ahead," Sage told him.

"How do I do it?"

"There are two stages. First, write down everything you know about yourself in your current life. Who you are, what you do, your talents and your perceived shortcomings. Don't try to make it sound better than it actually is. Just put in there what feels true."

"Alright, and then?"

"Now, write another description following the same blueprint, but this time, for your future self. Or rather, for the greatest version of your future self that you can think of."

"Like a fantasy?"

"No. Your *actual* vision of the future."

"You mean my goals, the actions I should take, and such?"

"Actions come second once you get clarity on *who* you are going to be. Then, take that vision of the future self and start living it *now*, thinking and feeling as your future self would. This will turbocharge your progress. Sometimes, you can achieve in a matter of days what may take years for someone who is not using this strategy."

"How so?"

"Because all times are intertwined. Although we usually can't experience this directly… In a certain sense, your future self already exists, just like your current and your past selves do. You haven't lived through it yet, but you're not separate from it. It's all within one quantum reality."

Mike squinted incredulously. "You're into quantum physics…?"

"Always have been," Sage answered with a line from a meme and favoured Mike with a broad smile. "It's the easiest way to explain things."

"Really? Quantum physics…is the *easiest* way?" Mike cocked his head ironically.

"Sometimes. Now, don't get distracted," Sage picked up his coffee cup. "Take what I'm saying as a working theory for now: all times are interconnected, so your future self already exists. This also means you can become your future self now, and bridge the gap faster."

"Alright."

"Start with writing your future personal story down. Avoid making it into an ego's wishlist. Quieten your mind and give yourself time to sit with it. Write only what *feels* true – a simple outline of what you sense you should be doing, and what kind of person you should be to make it happen."

"Right."

"Sometimes, it helps to imagine yourself at the end of your life, looking back – what path would make you feel that it was a life worth living? What would you have achieved in an ideal world that would give you a sense of completion and fulfilment? The sense of fully expressing yourself as a human being, and giving the world your greatest service and gifts? What would your most inspiring legacy be?"

Mike took a long exhale. "Wow... Loving those questions." He was scribbling as fast as his hand could manage. "I'll do this." Thinking about the homework gave him an unexplainable sense of lightness. "Can't wait."

"Good," Sage nodded. "Create a story that feels as real as the first one that you wrote, but which reflects your greatest *future* instead of your past. Most people are past-oriented, and that's their mistake. They allow their past to shape their future in its wake. A smart way of moving forward is to look into the future instead, and allow it to shape your present and your past."

"Shape my past...?"

"Yes. Once you start looking at your life through the eyes of your future self, the things and memories you're looking at will change. You will see new aspects of people, relationships and events that you'd never noticed before. You'll stop being interested in doing things that are not useful on your path." Sage smiled briefly. "It's like the ultimate productivity hack."

"What do you mean? How?"

"By the same token, as you grow older, you lose interest in the activities or toys you used to love as a toddler. Not because you discipline yourself to stay away from them, but simply because they are no longer relevant to who you currently are.

I have plenty of funny stories from my students..." Sage smiled lightly at his thoughts. "How they were amazed to discover they suddenly had no interest in wasting time on mindless activities, all by themselves. And started to move forward at full speed."

"Mindless like what, you mean doom scrolling? Or Netflix…"

"Anything procrastination related, really. Binge-watching TV, scrolling through social media, checking out all subreddits in sight… Generally, putting the important things off and then feeling bad or guilty about it. The success became inevitable because they'd made the forward thrust way stronger than the pushback. And so their greatest joy was to do things that served them on their path – the things that lead them to their greatest Purpose.

Some of them spent a lot of time and money on productivity coaches forcing them to do Pomodoro techniques, accountability, installing social media blockers and the like…" Sage creased his brow, "and never managed to achieve any lasting results with that. So they experience that 'wow effect' with how easy things become almost overnight. Always love hearing that…never gets old."

"I like that," Mike said readily. "My productivity is not too bad… but it could be better." He recalled the hours spent on Instagram, TikTok and Reddit and quickly pushed the thought away. "I'd like to move forward faster, too."

"Well, to move faster, you need to first decide *where* you're going," Sage told him. "Getting to live your Purpose is a lot like learning how to drive."

"Hmm?" Mike looked at his mentor questioningly. "What

do you mean?"

"Imagine that your Purpose is some actual place you want to get to. It's far away, and you've got a car. But here's the catch: you don't know how to drive. And there's no one else who could drive that car for you. You can't travel as a passenger in anyone else's, either. What would you do?"

"Well, I'd take some driving lessons," Mike ruffled his hair. "Seems like an obvious choice?"

"Right. So you learn the theory, get some driving practice and finally, you get a satnav or a map. Could you get there now?"

"Of course!"

"No, you can't."

"Why not…?"

"Because you need to know *where* you're going. The name of the place, or at least what it's supposed to look like. Otherwise, you'll just end up driving around in circles."

"Ah yes! Didn't think of that. My bad…" Mike snorted.

"See, your destination, your North Star, is the most important element. You can't get to a place, or achieve a goal, if you don't know what it is. Because the rest is flexible. As Miyamoto Musashi once said, 'There are many paths to the top of the mountain.' But you must first decide which mountaintop is yours."

"Got it." Mike smiled at the Musashi reference. "This reminds me, I started reading the Book of Five Rings before I travelled here."

"That's a good one," Sage nodded. "I just wish they had translated the title right. It's actually the Book of Five Elements. Musashi was influenced by Buddhism. The second character of the title – 'rin' – is a Buddhist word that means a 'level' or a 'stratum' and refers to the five basic elements: Earth, Water, Fire, Air, and Space."

"What? Interesting. That would make sense though, because each chapter is named after an Element… Why the 'five rings', then?"

"Because in secular Japanese, the same character means a wheel or a ring, and that's what the translator went for."

"Kind of weird."

"A lot of knowledge out there is misinterpreted and mistranslated," Sage responded with a note of melancholy. "It used to really bother me."

"Not anymore?"

"It still does, on some level. But I got used to it over the years." Sage paused. "Speaking of Musashi's books… Another good one is 'The Way of Walking Alone'."

"Never heard of that one."

"It's his last. He finished it just a week before he died. It's short and to the point. Close to the stoic philosophy."

"Wow, I'll check it out."

Sage nodded. "Remember your homework, too. Have a

go at mapping out your destination. We'll talk about the other forces next time."

Mike's homework notes:

"Study the four forces of the flight chart until you remember it."

"Write down what my best future version looks like, using the questions from today."

"Also describe what my current version of my personal story is that may be holding me back from my best life."

"Check out 'The Way of Walking Alone' by Musashi."

CHAPTER 11: YOUR PRIORITIES SHAPE YOUR LIFE

"You have to decide what your highest priorities are and have the courage—pleasantly, smilingly, non-apologetically, to say "no" to other things. And the way you do that is by having a bigger "yes" burning inside."
- Stephen Covey

"I kind of didn't want to come this time," Mike admitted sitting down, his face tense somewhat.

Sage looked at him and slightly cocked his head, but said nothing.

Mike shifted uncomfortably.

"It didn't work," he said. "I couldn't do it." He glanced down at his trainers, then at Sage again, and suddenly grinned. "I need coffee," he proclaimed. "Maybe that's what was missing."

"Quite possibly," Sage agreed lightly. "Well, let's get that sorted, then."

"I feel bad troubling that guy though… Trevor?"

"Tanner." Sage smiled and squinted his eyes. "He's not here today. He's got a business to run, after all."

"He's a business owner?" Mike flashed his eyebrows. "No way. I thought he was a kid…Oops, sorry. Like, early twenties or something."

"He's in his thirties."

"No way."

"He looked a lot older when he first started training with me," Sage said. "But he said he liked being young better."

Mike paused gathering his thoughts. "You can reverse aging?"

Sage looked at him and for a split moment, a mysterious glint flicked in his eye. "Amongst other things."

"You mean…" Mike twisted his mouth trying to make sense of what he heard. "You mean like biohacking or something?"

"No. Although a few nootropics here and there make things merrier. Speaking of which. Fancy a mushroom coffee? I know just the place."

"Wow, you know about it? Nice. Haven't had one in a while," Mike put his notebook back in his bag. "Sounds good."

"Alright then. Let's get some polyphenols, shall we?" Sage threw casually on his way out. He swiftly went down the stairs.

"What's that?" Mike followed him.

"Polyphenols are chemical compounds found in mushrooms and other plants…" Sage leant against the wall by the front door and opened a taxi app. "Some mushrooms have a lot of them. And other antioxidants... Combined, they can help reduce inflammation in the body. Arriving in 2 minutes," he lifted his eyes from his phone. "Reducing inflammation is one of the best things you can do for yourself, health-wise."

"For sure," Mike agreed, still perplexed at the unlikely array of things Sage seemed to know. He studied his mentor's slim silhouette propped against the wall and wondered, not for the first time, how old he actually was.

"Our cab is here," Sage announced opening the front door for Mike. "After you."

As soon as Mike stepped out, Sage swiftly opened one of the cupboards, took out a small pouch and slung it into his pocket. Next, he put on his sunglasses, winked to his reflection in the mirror and walked after his student into the midday heat.

The cafe was bright grey, spacey and cool from air-conditioning, like all places here. The decor presented an uncanny mixture between a sanctuary and a hotel lobby. Sage took a table in the corner.

"Show me your notes," he said after their coffees had arrived. "Let's see where you got stuck."

"I'm basically all things on the left," Mike admitted pointing at the Drag section of the 4 Forces chart. "I hate to say it but I still kind of care about what other people think. There's some fear as well... Not sure about traumas. Well, I wasn't a popular kid at school, so maybe that can count as... Didn't have many friends at that time. Or girls. It only came later. I guess I'm still trying to fit in and be accepted, somehow. Even with my current business. I'm not doing anything too crazy or creative. Just what I know that works. What other guys do out there." He paused. "Wow. I never shared such things before with anyone."

"You might have not been as fully aware of them as you are now."

"That's true." Mike paused again, looking at the chart. "My life circumstances are OK, I guess. Nothing is really holding me down, financially or otherwise. But these other two..." he moved his finger to the top and the right of the chart, "I struggle with these. I have a mentor and accountability now, but the rest of it is kind of fuzzy.

My tribe... Well, I can talk to other guys I know who also run businesses, but it's kind of shallow. Some of them are into self-development but it's either just endless productivity techniques – I mean, man, *how many* productivity techniques does one need? Lol – or it's some weird stuff I don't resonate with...like shrooms and such." He glanced at his coffee and snorted at the irony. "Not *this type* of shrooms."

He picked up his cup and continued, "I did some deep thinking about priorities, though. I realised I never thought about them in detail. I guess money was my priority... and health. Having a comfortable income and life. Supporting my family. Girls, when I was younger… A bit less so now. I have higher standards. I think that's it."

"You should write them down. In order of importance."

"Sure." Mike pulled his digital notepad closer to him and jotted down a short list, then showed it to Sage.

"Can you see what's missing?" Sage asked him.

Mike pulled the screen back and stared at it, rubbing the bridge of his nose. "No?"

"You put 'money' at the top. But you wouldn't be able to achieve that if you weren't willing to learn – just like what you're doing now. If learning wasn't one of your top priorities, you'd never hit your goals."

"That's right!" Mike clicked his fingers. "A good one." He added 'learning' close to the top of the list. "Anything else?"

"Yes. Safety."

"You mean, being financially secure?"

"Not only that. Remember what you said, you wanted other people to think of you a certain way. As a result, you censored yourself to be accepted. You built your business and your life not quite the way that would inspire you. Rather, it was what other people expected to see, and would approve of."

Mike set his lips. "I wish I could say that it wasn't true. But it is."

"That desire for safety is a sneaky enemy. It's often hard to spot it on your own. It tends to shapeshift and show up in unexpected ways. This is what has blocked your thinking about your greatest vision. It is also another reason why you're not quite as successful as you could be."

"Yeah… When I think about it, I always felt like there was a ceiling of sorts. Every time I got close to it, it felt as if something had pulled me back. I wasn't fully aware of it, until now. Like, every time there was a really big deal on the cards, or an opportunity to change direction or to expand, I'd find a way to talk myself out of it. Explaining to myself that I wasn't ready, or it wasn't the right time. Or I would just think it over until it was too late and the chance was gone." Mike cringed at some memories. "Was that for safety, though?"

"Yes. Your ego watches that you don't go out of your comfort zone, so it does everything it can to keep you small. See, if you start winning *really big*, you'll attract a lot of attention. And attention means that your perceived mistakes, weaknesses and shortcomings would be a lot more visible. The ego hates the idea of feeling exposed like that. So it would rather lock you in mediocrity."

"What? Excuse my language but that sucks! So it was doing that all this time behind my back?"

"Yes. And when you tried to imagine your greatest vision for yourself and your life, your ego blocked it."

"Right. I'm not going to put up with that. How do I tell it to shut up?" Mike twirled the stylus in his fingers.

"By going beyond the ego level and operating from there. Your mind is your property, so technically, you have the power to change any settings within it."

Mike squinted. "Technically?"

"It requires some work. And discipline."

"I can do that."

"You can. You just need to understand a couple of things."

Mike's homework notes:

"Have a look at what priorities your life currently reflects. Have you chosen them consciously or are they ideas copied over from others?"

"Make a list of my current priorities ordered in order of importance."

"How do my current priorities help me get closer to the life I want?"

"Are there any priorities (like safety) that are hindering my progress?"

THE SUPERHERO'S JOURNEY

CHAPTER 12:
THE BROKEN IKIGAI

"The more important a call or action to our soul's evolution, the more resistance we will feel toward pursuing it."
- Steven Pressfield

"Alright," Mike took his second serving of coffee, "how do I do it? I want to find something I'd feel passionate about doing while making some good profit from it. The 'ikigai' thing, you know."

"The ikigai chart doesn't work," Sage told him patiently. "I thought you might have figured it out by now."

"Well," Mike twisted his lips. "OK, so I went to a purpose coach before and that's what he told me. He got me to think about what I liked doing, what I was good at, and what was needed out there so I could make good money. That's how I came up with the idea for my current business."

Sage nodded. "I see. So that's how it started." He cocked his head and unexpectedly flashed an elvish smile. "And…how is it going?"

Mike glanced away, then back at Sage, like someone who got caught red-handed doing something stupid. "Well. It was actually good for a while," he said with a hint of defiance. "At the beginning, it was fun. It was exciting to see my biz grow, despite all the challenges. I loved the fact that I had to level up as a person, improving my mindset and all that." He paused. "Then at some point, it just became normal. And after that, it slowly started feeling pointless, more and more. Which is what brought me here."

Mike looked down at his notes, suddenly annoyed. Or maybe it was just frustration bubbling up, he couldn't tell.

"So then, why didn't you go back to that coach dude for another round?" Sage asked.

"That's a good question," Mike rubbed his chin with the stylus. "Hmm…" He went silent for a few moments, contemplating, then his eyes lit up with an insight. "I think I know why. Damn. Silly as it sounds… I was afraid. Only just realised it, though."

"Afraid of what?"

"That if I went back to him again, I'd end up hurling down another avenue that at first seemed great, only to discover that it wouldn't work in the long run. Like, I'd spend another chunk of my life pouring my energy into building something and then realising it was pointless, after all. Part of me kinda shrinks when I think about it."

"You're right," Sage told him lightly.

Mike gave him a somewhat startled look. "Right about what?"

"It would be exactly as you said."

"Hah. Glad I didn't do it, then."

"Yes. You saved yourself a lot of time and hassle. The ikigai chart doesn't work for finding your Purpose… It's not even designed in a way that could make it work." Sage said with a tone of resignation.

"What? Why? Everyone's talking about it…"

"I know. Almost two hundred thousand views for that hashtag, the last time I checked."

"Wow. Where is that?"

"TikTok. But a lie is still a lie even if thousands of people repeat it."

Mike ruffled his hair. "Hmm. Well, yes. What's wrong with it, though?"

"You've just experienced what's wrong," Sage answered with a half-smile.

"I guess, but… I still don't understand why."

"That concept is an ego-bait," Sage told him. "The diagram

looks pretty, too. An easy sell. It promises that you can stay cosy in your comfort zone and get everything you want, somehow. Purpose is the opposite of that."

"Hmm…"

"Purpose is not something you feel good about straight away. In fact, people often resist it, especially at the start. They get stuck at the 'refusal of the call' stage because of their fears and insecurities. It takes perseverance, and usually a good mentor, to succeed."

"Alright, but what's wrong with using the ikigai diagram to get there?"

"It won't take you there," Sage said plainly. "Firstly, the question shouldn't be about 'what you're good at' because if you're already good at something that's a lesson learnt. Your soul *doesn't want you* to keep repeating it. It wants you to move forward. So if you keep doing only what you're good at for long enough, you'll start feeling empty and fed up."

"Yes, I can see that."

"There should be an element of growth and challenge – and not any odd obstacle but a type of challenge that forces you to reevaluate the way you see yourself and the world. That's why creating any business can be exciting at the start, even if it's not aligned – it's the factor of learning and growth that makes it interesting. But once you get into the stage where you're doing okay, you stagnate there. There doesn't seem to be any way forward."

"Yes."

"So here's the first point – your Purpose requires of you to constantly become better, as a continued process. And you know you're on the right track when working on mastering something feels *uncomfortable*. You *will* start enjoying it with time, and loving it – but that will come much later. So instead of asking, 'What are you good at?', or 'What do you enjoy doing?' the question should be 'What secretly excites you but you wouldn't dare to go anywhere near it?' Only this one will give you the right answer. Everything else will burn out pretty quickly."

"Love it!" Mike declared while taking notes.

"There's a book about this I can recommend, it's called High Purpose Code. Check it out."

"Sounds good," Mike wrote down the title and circled it. "Will do."

"And the 'excitement' part, it's never about a selfish pleasure," Sage continued. "It's about how you can offer the greatest, most valuable and meaningful service to the world, based on *who you are*. Which brings us to the second point."

"Which is?" Mike lifted his gaze from the screen.

"Most people don't know who they actually are. Or rather, they don't remember. And so they have no clear idea of what they like, or what they are capable of."

Mike tossed the stylus in his fingers, contemplating. "What do you mean?" He asked finally.

"Well, if you don't know someone, you don't know what they like, right?"

"Uhm, yes."

"That applies to yourself as well."

"But I do know who I am!" Mike protested.

"You think you do, but you don't," Sage told him matter-of-factly. "Otherwise, you would be living your Purpose already. You are not who you think you are. That's why you can't yet properly answer the question about what excites you or what motivates you, deep down."

"Ah."

"It's not directly your fault that you ended up here. Our society makes it so. You know your ego story, but not who you truly are, outside of it."

"Do *you* know?"

"Yes," Sage looked at Mike and a strange, infinite expression flickered in his gaze. "It's not that complicated."

CHAPTER 13: REMEMBERING WHO YOU ARE

"Do not seek pleasure for its own sake."
- Miyamoto Musashi, The Way of Walking Alone

The late afternoon sun was warm and hazy. Sage and Mike left the cafe and went back to take a cosy spot by the pool. The weather was perfect for it.

"Look at the chart," Sage said. "See where it says here on the right things like 'freedom, power, money and Purpose – aka a lucrative career?'"

"Yes."

"If you ask people what they want, nearly all answers will be a combination of these."

"Well, of course! What else can you want from life."

Sage threw Mike an ironic glance. "Why are you here,

then? You have all of those."

"Hmm... Okay, fair enough." Mike squinted and folded his arms behind his head. "But that's most people's drive."

"Indeed, it is," Sage said. "But they don't realise that they are missing the main point while chasing consequences."

"What do you mean?"

"All those things – money, freedom, influence and such – are merely the consequences of being true to who you are. In other words, they are the 'side effects' of following your Purpose and serving the world greatly. Just like a shining lightbulb is a consequence of flipping the light switch."

"You mean, the rewards?"

"For an outsider, yes. But the real reward is to understand who you are on a higher level, and to live as your true self. Believe me, that feeling is more empowering than millions of dollars, and more addictive than a drug," Sage smiled. "Words fail to convey what it's like. It's best to be experienced. It's what we all secretly want deep down. That effortless, blissful flow. Because the only true power and freedom are those that come from within. The rest are smoke and mirrors."

"Ah, so that's why it says 'self-realisation' at the bottom there."

"Yes. See, if you grow on the purely mundane level and simply maximise your skills, expertise and connections, you'll earn financial freedom, followers, recognition and whatever else you want in return—"

"Yes."

"—But that's never going to be enough because you're only partly a physical being. The other, spiritual part of you—your soul—also has its needs. It will be nudging you and make you restless until you remember that.

It's a similar urge that makes a seed germinate and become a plant. In basic terms, that's what self-realisation is about."

Sage paused watching the dance of light on the water. "If you chase money for money's sake or impact for impact's sake, you'll end up getting that and nothing else. It will still be the same limited, 'coffee bean' version of you, only with piling up responsibilities and no way out. If you look behind the facade of many influencers, you'll see what I mean. The 'Now what?' question."

"Yeah, I can relate to that."

"It's because while you're busy chasing reflections, your true, deepest desire remains unsatisfied. And as time goes by, frustration wells up. You can imagine it as if when you're hungry, you only got occasional snacks instead of a proper meal. For years."

"Wow, that would suck."

"You see, becoming wealthy or famous can't be your Purpose, just like eating good food can't be your Purpose. They are means to an end; simply the tools that your soul can use to fulfil its mission here.

What you want is to *actually* satisfy that desire rather than keep distracting yourself… And the only way to achieve that is to level up."

"How do I do it?"

"By remembering who you are, and embodying that truth. And then creating an exceptional life out of it. A life truly worth living."

Sage paused. "Some people are lucky in that they don't fully forget," he continued. "They have a vision of what they could become, which comes to them in dreams or as a childhood memory. Sometimes, it's simply a 'silent knowing'. Akin an instinct that brings the birds of passage home from across the oceans. But not everyone is like that."

"I see." Mike looked contemplatively into the distance. The sun glitter from the water reflected on his face and chest. "Well, I did fancy being a superhero as a kid," he smiled lightly. "But otherwise, there's no clear vision that I can recall."

"That's not a problem," Sage replied assuringly. "That's what blueprints are for. You learn the principles then apply them in a way that works best for you." An elvish glint flashed in his eye. "Imagine copying a proven sales funnel, then tweaking it to make your own."

Mike snorted. "No way you just said that… Well then, are the conversion rates good?"

"Excellent."

Mike shook his head. *Who is this guy, honestly...?!* He rubbed the bridge of his nose. "Alright, so what's that blueprint?" he asked.

"The Timeless Way," Sage said simply.

"What?" Mike flashed his eyebrows. "Like on that scroll you have? The one I saw when I first walked in?"

"Yes. It's a reminder. Great for meditation, too." Sage leant back on his sunlounger and threw his hands behind his head. "The Timeless Way is the most straightforward way to self-realisation that I know. And I've seen...many."

"Why is it called that?"

"Because those principles are timeless. They are as true for you as for the scholars hundreds of years ago, and for those who may want to retrace our steps centuries from now."

"Will you be around to guide them?" Mike couldn't help himself.

"Maybe."

"So... you... you're immortal, right? Aren't you?" Mike finally voiced the question that had been burning in his mind for so long.

"We all are..." Sage answered with melancholy. "From a certain point of view. Now, you've got a choice," he turned to Mike changing his tone. "Choose wisely."

"Yes?" Mike focused, anticipating some mind-boggling riddle.

"We can either end our session for today… Or I'm going to order some food," Sage squinted ironically. "It's nearly evening."

"Uhm, yes!" Mike snorted taken off guard. "Food would be great. I can keep going. I'm really curious to hear the rest of this."

CHAPTER 14: THE MAN'S SECRET TO SELF-REALISATION

"In order to have what you really want, you must first be who you really are.'"
– Tim S. Grover, New York Time Bestselling Author of 'Winning And Relentless'

"Your worth is not of this world because it was given to you from beyond this world."
– Heiko Kern

"It's pretty simple," Sage said. "You'll just need some determination and discipline, like with working out. At first, it's more work than fun. Also, your old self will fight back and try to make you forget again."

"Good luck with that," Mike sniffed derisively. "It can try all it wants. When I set myself a goal, I don't stop until I get there." He briefly flexed his biceps for proof. "End of story." He grabbed a glass of orange juice and quaffed down half of it. "So, what's the blueprint?"

"I'll give you a step-by-step strategy in a bit. First, you start with knowing, deeply, three core truths. The Three Fundamentals. Without them, you'd have a hard time realising your Purpose. They're very straightforward, although many find them hard to accept."

"I'm all ears," Mike said, his stylus at the ready above the screen.

"The first one is that you're a man."

Mike snorted. "Well, I know *that*."

"Really?" Sage lifted his brow. "What does it mean to be a man, then?"

"Sure, so... It means..." Mike's voice trailed off as he stared at the water in front of him, illuminated by the lights from below. 'Boys don't cry,' a line from childhood popped into his mind, followed by the dress-up scene from Family Guy, then instantly after, a battle scene from the Gladiator. His mind was into playing its annoying games, again. "I guess, it means protecting... someone important," he said finally. "Like your tribe or family."

"Is that it? Women can protect their families, too."

"Well, yeah...but also... Leading by example."

Sage didn't seem impressed. "Is that it?" He asked again. "A hunter-fighter caveman type of psychology?"

Mike frowned and finished his orange juice in a somewhat flustered manner. "No! Of course not. There's a lot more."

"Let's hear it." Sage passed him the jug to refill his glass.

"Well…there's also… Being a good husband, maybe? Or a good dad."

"It does sound noble, doesn't it?" Sage looked pensively into the distance. "And with such temptingly low barriers to entry, it becomes a favourite cop-out for many guys. Especially those who try to run from answering the 'What does it mean to be a man?' question. Some also try to use it as a substitute for Purpose."

"But it *can* be someone's Purpose, no?"

Sage shook his head somewhat wearily. "Think about it this way. If our lives' objectives could be reduced to protecting our territory, building up supplies, and looking after our offspring, then how would we be any different from animals? We wouldn't even need a brain more complex than that of a squirrel." He twisted a corner of his lips. "And yet, we are a lot more advanced than that."

"So then…"

"It *can* be an expression of how you choose to serve, sure. If you've found the One and it feels right – it could be part of your quest towards discovering who you are. But it's not a 'one size fits all' answer, even though it's being pushed as such. People are all different. Some paths are meant to be shared, others are not. Society doesn't care about such nuances, though. It wants new workers and new taxpayers. So there's a lot of social pressure to get married at a certain age...usually way before boys have a chance to become men, truly. Before they learn what being a man really means. Deep down, they hope that becoming a father would magically do the trick, somehow."

"Yeah, I've noticed that... with my friends and some other people I've met," Mike said.

"You know what's worse?"

"What?"

"Creating your identity based on that. As a man, don't ever let any social responsibilities define you. At the end of the day, it's only one of the many roles we can play. Tying your sense of identity to your income, your marital status or your position is a very insecure place to be. Can you see why? You'll be compelled to put all your energy and effort into keeping up that thing you've built your identity around.

Firstly, that would stop you from growing as a person, making you feel stuck. And secondly, nothing in the external world is truly in your hands. That means that if you lose that position, that relationship, or that income – everything, including your sense of masculinity, crumbles. Because you've forgotten that you're more than your role. That's a long way of saying that none of those things could be your Purpose."

"I see."

"Here's another aspect to it. As an entrepreneur, it means

that you're an older soul, so your playing field tends to be a lot bigger. Your talent and energy may be needed globally, and having dependants early on may slow you down. You should listen to your gut and go with what feels right. And in any case, never start a family as a cop-out."

"What do you mean?"

"If you're not whole within yourself and you don't know what you stand for, a partner or a child isn't going to fix it on your behalf. They surely can serve as a distraction from the void inside, though. Temporarily, anyway. Which is how many guys approach it, sadly."

"Wow. This would be a hard pill to swallow for some. Having their ideas shattered."

"I know. But the ability to be honest with yourself is the greatest flex. And in the long run, it hurts less than doing the wrong things for the wrong reasons. Deep down, those guys know they are *not* where they're meant to be in life. If you look closely, plenty of them are visibly depressed."

"Uhmm yeah… Have *you* ever been married?"

"Not in this lifetime, no. My path is a Way of Walking Alone," Sage smiled lightly.

"That sounded strange."

"It's the title of one of Musashi's books. I told you about it earlier."

"No, I mean the 'lifetime' part."

"Ah yes, we come here more than once. There's no way to fit all lessons into a single life. Imagine some not even being around for long enough to enter adulthood… But anyway, we've digressed. Since you say you know you're a man, tell me what it means. Outside of any social roles."

"Sure. Alright…" Mike was determined to nail this impromptu test. "Hmm… You don't copy anyone else." He chewed his lip but then suddenly remembered. "The force!" He exclaimed. "The centrifugal force. You need to be a tornado." He looked pleased with himself now.

"Correct. But what does it practically mean?" Sage kept drilling in.

"It means… No hiding! You should have the courage to show up. And carve your own path," Mike's voice was slightly less certain. "And something about being the Chosen One." He twisted his mouth.

"That's right," Sage told him. "Although you don't sound like someone who actually owns that."

"I find it hard to connect the dots in my mind," Mike admitted.

"It's a typical reaction from the ego. I warned you that your ego wouldn't like you moving forward."

"Uhm, yes."

"No worries, let's recap it, then. The masculine polarity is the electric principle of the universe. In simple words, it's a force that *makes things happen.* It doesn't wait for perfect times and opportunities – it creates them. Its keywords are *autonomy, willpower* and *control*."

"Willpower as in 'discipline'?"

"Discipline is a side effect of focus. Willpower is what fuels that focus. It's a foundation of self-governance and a goal-oriented mindset. The masculine *influences* rather than being influenced, inside and out."

"Could you give me an example?"

"Sure. You know how some people say things like, 'I'm this way because my parents, my upbringing or my circumstances made me so'? or, 'I can't do this or that because of what happened in the past'?"

"Oh, lots of them."

"Being on the receiving end of things is the Lunar – feminine – dynamic. It's not negative per se, but for a man, it can be hugely disempowering. Some people take it to the extreme and develop a victim's mindset. They move through life like boats without a rudder, drifting on with no clear plan and no goal ahead. They let other people and circumstances define and control them."

"I see."

"As a man, you should evaluate the demands and ideas that come your way, and reject those that don't support your key goals: evolving as a person while offering a great service to the world with your expertise or business. Be strict. It doesn't matter whether those influences come from your parents, friends, social media, or from your own bad memories and traumas. Your mind is your domain, so you must have the ultimate say on what stays in there. To be aligned with your polarity, always cultivate these two: autonomy and control."

"Why is it important to be in tune with your polarity, though? Just curious. They are both equally important, right?"

"Yes, but to live your Purpose is to live 'as designed'. Since you're a man, you must show up as one. The opposite polarity weakens your energy and your mind. The further you go down that path, the more your life closes in on you. You end up as a victim of other people's opinions and circumstances. Another way to put it: breaking away from your polarity is a fast track towards becoming a pathetic lifeform."

Mike snorted at the movie reference. "By polarity you mean gender?"

"They tend to coincide, although not always. For you, they are in sync. Choosing to live the way you were meant to live is the best choice you can make."

"Agreed."

Sage nodded. "Alright, now that you've got clarity on that, let's talk about being in control."

"Let's," Mike said readily, scooping a handful of chunky potato chips from the box. He wiped his fingers on a paper tissue and picked up his stylus again. 'Control' he wrote on the new page and drew a circle around the word.

"It's one of the three keywords, as you remember," Sage said. "But many guys don't understand what it actually means. They tend to think 'control' implies having power over others, as in being a control freak."

Mike ruffled his hair. "But really, it's about having control over your mind and your emotions like the stoics say, right?"

"The 'rule your mind or it will rule you' axiom is still as true today as it was at the times of Horace," Sage replied. "A deliberate response trumps a knee-jerk emotional reaction every time. This is more about self-governance, though: you stand your ground regardless of the storms that rage around."

"So what does it mean to be in control?"

"You won't like the answer," Sage flashed a smile.

"What..?" Mike blinked at him, puzzled.

"It means accepting your mission as the 'Chosen One'," Sage told him. "It's about being the protagonist in your own story. In other words, be willing to accept responsibility for how your life unfolds. Realise that if you want to transform your life – your world – it's *on you*. Regardless of your circumstances, the economy, or the opportunities you get. You have what it takes to succeed on that quest. But it starts with accepting your mission."

"Oh, alright," Mike nodded thoughtfully. It all suddenly made sense. "I think I get it now."

"It's about being deliberate with where you're going. Become autonomous – diversify your investments, control your sources of income and the direction in which your business scales – and you're one-third of the way there."

"Only one-third?"

"Yes. The second element of being in control is managing your mind. This goes beyond the stoic mindset of standing your ground and not letting your emotions or the expectations of others sway you. It's about how you show up externally, too. Approach your life and business like you'd approach a battlefield. Keep your skills current, and sharp, and make sure that they serve you well. Get into the habit of 'deliberate practice' with learning and levelling up. Become formidable when it comes to gaining knowledge and insight. Do your own research and develop your own judgement, regardless of what others say."

"Great. And what's the third one?"

"The last one is your paradigm. You must see yourself as the centre of power in your world. Like the sun surrounded by planets. Those 'planets' are ideas, people, possibilities, events. We spoke about it, remember? You choose what to give attention to – and whatever you give attention to, manifests and grows. You craft your life by pulling things out of the multitude of possibilities and making them a reality; making their wave function collapse a certain way."

"Manifestation?"

"You can call it that. Mastering this skill is every man's responsibility. Reality bending is the third part of you exercising your sense of masculinity and control. It gives you strength."

"This is great," Mike muttered while taking notes, his stylus sliding fast on the screen. "I'm glad we didn't cut today short. Do you teach manifestation, too?"

"I do," Sage said matter-of-factly. "It's going to be in the second part of your training. The practice part."

"Hmm?"

"Remember the analogy with learning to drive? It's like that with getting to your Purpose as well. First, you must understand some theory. Then, I'll show you how to put that knowledge into practice. And after that, you'll get to design your own 'roadmap'."

Mike nodded. "Awesome. Look forward to it."

"Alright, so to sum it up," Sage said. "To live as a man means to go forward and make things happen in accordance with your will. The masculine polarity is a creative one. You mustn't settle. You can't just 'accept what is'. Instead, craft a reality that nourishes your soul. Design it. Own it. Call forth out of the sea of possibilities. The closer you're aligned with that dynamic, the more your personal power will grow. Your greatest legacy is in the strength of your presence, as well as the support, inspiration and truth that you share with others."

"Love it. I'll get this printed out as a reminder," Mike said.

"Great idea," Sage nodded and looked up at the sky. "Let's go on the roof," he suggested suddenly. "The stars are out."

Mike Homework Notes:

"The masculine polarity is the electric principle of the universe. In simple words, it's a force that *makes things happen*. It doesn't wait for perfect times and opportunities – it creates them. Its keywords are *autonomy, willpower* and *control*."

"Meditate on what being a man truly means. What do each of these keywords mean for me personally?"

"See how you can show up in your life as the protagonist. What would it be like to go through life being the Chosen One for my unique mission? How would I think and act from that perspective?"

CHAPTER 15: TRANSCENDING THE LEVELS OF CONSCIOUSNESS

"Who you think you are and who you actually are, are two very different things."

– J. H. Tepley

"Let's grab our drinks and go," Sage got up snatching his glass of juice.

"What? Why?" Mike blinked at him, confounded.

"An old habit," Sage replied as he walked across the patio; he looked back and stopped waiting for Mike to catch up.

Mike sighed, glanced at the pool quivering with liquid light, gathered his writing utensils and joined Sage.

"Back in the day," Sage told him nostalgically as they went

up the staircase, "it was too hot in the daytime, so we looked forward to the nightfall. After sunset, we'd go up on the roofs to eat, drink, catch up with friends, and look at the stars. Still love it now."

"When was that? You mean, here?"

"No. A while back… about two and a half thousand years ago. Ancient Media and Babylonia. I was from Media myself, but I travelled to Babylon a few times."

"You did…WHAT?" Mike gaped at him.

"I travelled to Babylon a few times," Sage repeated, unruffled. "I've been to the Marduk temple there as well. It was huge… I told you we lived more than once," he added ironically, noticing Mike's expression. "Maybe one day, I'll finally earn a dingir before *my* name, too." He sniffed at his own joke and toasted the sky with his glass.

"What's a dignir?"

"Dingir," Sage corrected. "A star-shaped sign in cuneiform writing. It used to be put in front of the names of the immortals, kings and heroes."

"Neat. I should get one."

Sage raised his glass again. "Go for it."

The vast dome of stars opened above them, marred at the edges by the brightness of city lights. Sage gestured to the chairs inside the pergola in the middle. Instead of going there, however, he suddenly took a few steps forward and jumped on the stone parapet of the roof, with the dexterity of a ninja.

"Hey! Watch out!" Mike gasped taken by surprise.

"I have a good sense of balance," Sage told him without turning his head. His silhouette darkened against the night sky.

Mike could swear he saw a faint golden glow around Sage's figure. But then he blinked and the glow was gone.

"The Timeless Way," Sage said picking up the conversation from before, "is a path of becoming who you really are. That's what all seekers, mystics and yogis throughout human history have been looking for. And now the answer can be yours, too. Which is – you can't live your Purpose without knowing who you are, and without embodying that truth."

"Hmm…"

"I know," Sage turned to him and smiled lightly. "Right from the start, you hoped I'd just give you charts and diagrams, and daily routines to boot, and leave it at that."

"Well, yeah, actually. I did."

"You'll get your action steps," Sage assured him, "but later. You see, none of that stuff would work if you don't get the Fundamentals first. It's like building a house. You start by laying the foundations before adding the walls and any pretty details. It's not going to be stable otherwise."

"The Fundamentals? Ah, yeah. How many are there, again?"

"Three," Sage finished his orange juice and jumped down; then headed to the pergola. "You can see them as artefacts in a game. You've got to collect all three to unlock a new level. Your quest is going pretty well, though – you've scored one already."

"Sorry, which one was it? We spoke about so much stuff."

"Being a man."

"Hah, yes. That one was awesome."

"The other two are pretty useful, too," Sage paused for a moment. "Tired?"

"Not at all," Mike said hotly. "Excited to keep going. So what's the second Fundamental?"

"This," Sage said stretching out his hand before him, palm up. A small ball of golden fire flared above his hand then faded slowly.

Mike flinched, his eyes widening in shock. "What… was THAT? Did you just—?" He rubbed his face. "Was the juice spiked?!"

Sage gave a short chortle. "It wasn't."

"WHAT DID YOU JUST DO??" Mike demanded. "Is it some kind of a trick?"

"No," Sage said calmly. "I'll do it again, more slowly. Look." A golden sphere appeared above his palm once more.

For a split second, Mike thought he should probably be scared, but the excitement took over. "What is that…?" he asked in a whisper.

"The answer to your question," Sage said, making the energy sphere fade away. "We're only partially physical beings. Really, we are a union of human and divine. If you want to succeed on your quest, you need to discover and embody that part of you, just as you learnt about what being a man means." The golden fire flickered in his eyes now.

"No way you just did that…" Mike shook his head. "Come on, that wasn't real."

Sage looked at him ironically. "You want to be convinced?"

"Well… Yeah! I do."

"Alright, get up, then," Sage said with the same ironic smile on his lips but his eyes were dangerous and narrow. "Since you asked for it."

What am I packing myself into? A worried thought scurried through Mike's mind but once again, excitement and curiosity had won. He got up and stood opposite Sage.

"Stretch your arm out in front of you," Sage directed, coming closer. "Now, hold it still and don't let me push it down."

Mike grinned sarcastically, watching his mentor trying to push down his burly arm with merely two of his fingers. Mike's arm remained still like a rock.

"See, this is what happens when we interact matter to matter," Sage said. "Now watch." He did a slight movement with his hand, almost imperceptible, then pressed on Mike's wrist with two fingers as before.

This time, Mike's arm dropped down, powerless, as if it were an arm of a child.

"WHAT?!" Mike stared at his arm that dared to betray

him just like that, as though all those hours at the gym meant nothing. "How did you—?!"

"Don't worry, you'll get your strength back. In fact, do you want me to make you stronger than before?" Sage squinted elvishly.

"Yes."

"Sure, here we go," Sage did something again then pushed Mike's arm down with both his hands. Mike didn't even flinch. His muscles now felt as solid as a concrete block, unmovable.

"Nice…" Mike uttered appreciatively, flexing his arm. "But…how?"

"Your body is controlled by the electrical impulses from your brain, which is, in turn, controlled by your mind," Sage said. "And your mind is energy. To put it simply, energy comes before matter." He gestured to sit. "If you understand that, you'll understand how to be truly efficient in life." He paused and looked at the sky, then continued, "People tend to get it the wrong way round. They think they are bodies with a soul. Most will look in the mirror and say, "That's me". But the truth is, you're not your body. You're not even your mind. Your 'true self' is an energy being. Try it," he said to Mike. "First, make your mind empty of thoughts for a few moments."

"Easier said than done," Mike told him. "I could never do it, even in meditation. My mind keeps racing, no matter what."

"Just focus your attention on both your wrists at the same time, and the inner chatter will stop," Sage said. "If you want, you can wiggle your wrists a bit to make focusing easier."

"Neat!" Mike sounded excited. "Whoa, not a single thought, just like that. That's a cool hack."

Sage nodded. "Now, stay present in that silence, see what comes up."

"Alright, now what?" Mike asked after a few moments.

"When you had no thoughts running through your head, was there a sense of 'I'? The sense of your personal story?"

"Hmm… Actually, no."

"What about the sense of your body?"

"No. I didn't even feel it. Like if it didn't exist."

"So what remained, then?" Sage asked.

"Just kind of… a sense of… watching? Being present. An awareness."

"Great. And where was that located?"

"What do you mean, where?"

"Well, you know where your body is in space?"

"Of course."

"Now in that awareness state, while you didn't feel your body, *where* were you?"

"Good question. I'm not sure. I'll have to try again to check." Mike closed his eyes and fell silent for a few moments. "Weird.

It feels kind of like you're a liquid that got spilt. Like, you go everywhere at once. I was here with you on the roof, but also kind of watching myself sitting there with you, and being in this city in general. And it felt…peaceful. I guess the most peaceful I've ever been."

"What you've experienced was pure awareness. This is the core of your being, the most fundamental part of you. It exists beyond our world, and it's limitless and eternal. Everything else comes and goes."

"What do you mean, comes and goes?"

"We function on different planes of reality. For the physical level, we have our body and a level of the mind that governs it – the carnal, or the body-mind. On a more subtle level, we have a soul, and its soul-mind. Then beyond that, we have our conscious or ego mind which for most people is a focal point of their identity. Spoiler alert: if you allow your identity to be rooted in that level, you'll experience a lot of pain and struggle in life."

"Where should it be, then?"

"One step up. Beyond the conscious mind, there's a level that in psychology is referred to as the Superconscious. This is the level of the Higher Self. Your Higher Self is what connects your pure awareness with the reality of this world.

By itself, awareness is not suited to function here. It takes no action and has no desires. It only observes and is aware of what it is observing at that moment. It's the level that Transcendental

Meditation, and other forms of meditation, aim to take you to. The sense of 'I am that I am' in an eternal Now. I call it 'State Zero' – because it has zero thoughts, zero emotions, and zero memories. It's not good to remain in that state for too long, especially if you haven't been trained for it... But in short bursts, it can offer a useful shift in perspective.

That awareness is a constant process that runs in the background whether you're conscious of it or not. It is the anchor of our existence. Everything else, every other level of the mind we have, is essentially, a reflection of it.

Reflections come and go. Once this life runs its course, you'll get another body, and another ego-mind, but the core of who you are will remain. You can see it like playing a computer game. You can create different characters with different features, but *the one who is playing* remains behind the screen. No matter what happens to your character – even if it drowns or gets shot – that 'not affected. You can choose to respawn it, if you like, and carry on. That's the position of awareness."

"Wow, alright. So hold on, we're kind of immortal, then?"

"Yes, in a way, we are," Sage smiled. "I told you. Our core essence is immortal... as energy cannot be created nor destroyed. But the reflections it casts are perishable."

"What do you mean? What are those reflections?"

"Projections of awareness on different levels of reality. These are the four different levels we just spoke about. Your physical body, your soul, your ego-mind and your Higher Self.

A human being is not a monolith but rather a unit consisting of these interconnected elements. To understand that better, you need to understand first how our reality works. Hmm… Ever seen a crepe cake?"

"Yeah, of course. Why?"

"It's just an analogy of what our world is like. It's got layers. They are multidimensional, of course… But for simplicity, you can imagine them being stuck on top of each other. They have different properties, but together they make up one whole. You can see yourself kind of piercing through them, so you're functioning on all levels at the same time."

"Wow, fascinating. How are they so different, though?"

"Here's how it works. Picture our Solar System with the Sun in the middle. The light is brighter the closer you get to the Sun. The further away, the more the light dissipates."

"Yes."

"Well, our reality is a bit like that. Everything is put in motion by the universal Light that flows from the Source. Unlike the physical light though, as it travels further away, rather than dissipates, it solidifies.

The further away, the more physical its creations become. The closer to the Source, the more rarefied the forms. All creation, including manifestation, happens in this way.

A blueprint is created on a higher plane, then it gradually solidifies until it eventually appears in physical reality. This is why if you picture yourself in a certain way in meditation, before long, your body and your mind will start changing accordingly. Arnold Schwarzenegger used this principle to grow muscles faster, he said—"

"—That's seriously cool. I'll try that!" Mike rubbed his chin imagining what else could be possible.

"Here's the most important quest if you want to align with your Purpose… You need to learn how to access your Higher Self, and control your energy to change reality around you. Humans refer to that skill as 'superpowers'." Sage's lips curved slightly. "But it's a must, really. Without it, you can never reach your full potential."

Mike gave out a switching breath. "So… Can you do more of that reality bending stuff?"

"If there's a need," Sage answered in an everyday tone of voice. "Levitation is off the cards, though."

"Can I… do it, too?" Mike asked slowly.

"Of course."

Mike steepled his fingers and rested his head on them. For a moment, he remained silent but then his shoulders shook with suppressed laughter until he was sniggering out loud. "So…" he said turning to Sage, "you… you *actually meant it* with the Avengers thing."

Sage smiled. "You can put it that way. The Avengers, the Jedi… whatever resonates."

"I'm in! Man, I'm sooo in," Mike was still choking on laughter. "Sorry, I don't… mean to be disrespectful or anything.

It's just… something I've always wanted." He sniffed and shook his head. "I wanted it so bad as a kid. But thought it was impossible."

"Kids often have a clearer view of things," Sage said. "They still remember that we are half divine creatures…and we should live as such. You can imagine that Higher Self as a superhuman…or an archangel version of you. A bit like what you see in superhero movies," Sage winced slightly at the cheesy comparison, "but more profound. More real. This should give you an idea, though. Who you *truly* are is very different from how you currently see yourself. You need to rewrite your identity, your personal story, to reflect your truth. That's how you win big, and create an epic impact that changes lives. At our core, we are eternal. Timeless."

"Like the Timeless Way?"

"Yes. The truth of who we are never changes." Sage seemed suddenly pensive. "You need to understand this. Really, deeply understand this." He paused. "Unless you live and function as the full expression of self, you'll never feel 'enough'. Most likely, you'd constantly plateau and feel depressed, no matter what else you do. It's just how it works."

"Got it. So… Will you show me the way of the Force?" Mike grinned. "It's strong with me, I'm sure."

"Absolutely," Sage smiled back at him. "But speaking of the Force…let's talk about the third Fundamental first."

"Ah, yes. Nearly forgot. What is it?"

"The last shift in perception you need to be able to 'live as designed' is to see yourself as an *active force*."

"What does that mean?"

"It means that firstly, you're an action-oriented being. You need to remember this, especially when things get comfortable. You can't allow yourself to get complacent and stagnate. Your life dynamic requires you to keep moving forward, to new challenges and new achievements. You must never stop learning and growing."

Mike curved his lips in acknowledgement. "That's straightforward enough."

"And secondly, it means that you're an agent of change in the world. You see, everything is interlinked. We are submersed in one massive quantum soup. What you do, say, or even think, has an impact on the people around you, even if neither you nor them are aware of it. For example, by levelling up, you help others rise. And if you drag yourself down, other people will be affected as well. You can look at it as a form of quantum entanglement. Quantum reality is a bit wild like that."

"I see."

Seeing the confusion on Mike's face, Sage added, "Imagine throwing a pebble into still water. Ripple will spread out in circles from the point of impact."

"Yes."

"Your individual consciousness creates ripples through spacetime as it touches the universal consciousness we all exist in. The best way is to experience this directly, but it takes a bit of time. Just become aware of it for now. Imagine yourself as a centre of power in your world. Like a Sun, around which your entire world rotates."

"Hold on, we spoke about it earlier, right?" Mike looked up his notes to make sure.

"Yes. This is another aspect of manifestation as well. Your personal frequency 'bends' the reality around you reflecting what you project, reflecting those 'ripples'." Sage paused. "The bottom line is, you must *know* that your mere presence makes a difference. It's hard to make the wrong decisions once you have this knowledge rooted firmly in your mind."

"I see…" Mike leant back in his chair, throwing his hands behind his back. The sky was serene and limitless above him. That was what he felt right now, too. Serene and limitless. Even though there was a *lot* to think about. "I'll need to think about it all," he finally said.

"I know," Sage replied. "I've got something for you, by the way."

"What's that?" Mike threw him a curious glance.

"Something that will help you remember who you are," Sage said, handing Mike a little pouch. Inside, there was a thin orange bracelet, an exact copy of the one Sage had on his wrist. "The way our mind works," he explained, "is that we tend to forget important things quickly. Use this as an anchor, to help you stay on track."

Mike's homework notes:

"To be the center of power in your world – go through the medi warmup (video in the student library or https://newerasuperhero.com/medi-warmup). Then, imagine yourself as a Sun around which your entire world rotates. Feel the power of attention and choice radiating from you into your life. Realise that all events, people are circumstances are there because you pulled them in, by choice."

"Meditate to feel what being a higher version of yourself would be like. How would he think, feel, act, and see the world? Then live it out in your everyday life. Use the bracelet as an anchor. Notice, how day by day, the way you feel about yourself and the way you interact with others, changes."

"To merge with the Higher Self faster, use the Instant Transcendence meditation track. This also allows you to go into the state of awareness."

"Get clear on the Three Fundamentals for Purpose."

"A hack to delve into the pure awareness quickly when outside is to imagine that you don't exist. You can imagine your body or your ego disappearing, but awareness always remains there. Then you can just tune into that state to observe and rest. This is a very useful mode especially when something annoys or frustrates you. Nothing has power over awareness, but awareness has power over everything. Don't remain in that state for too long in one go."

THE SUPERHERO'S JOURNEY

CHAPTER 16: UNLOCKING YOUR GOD STATE

"To say 'I'm God' spoken by the ego-self is a statement of grandiose megalomania. Spoken as a soul or Higher Self, it's a statement of self-realization."
- Frederick Dodson

"When you examine the lives of the most influential people who have ever walked among us, you discover one thread that winds through them all. They have been aligned first with their spiritual nature and only then with their physical selves."
- Albert Einstein

"I feel different," Mike declared as he stepped onto the patio and joined Sage by the pool. "I mean, since we last spoke."

There was, indeed, some air of change about him; his movements lighter and smoother than usual; even his face looked changed somewhat.

"I didn't really do anything," he continued. "Well, I did think about what you told me then – and suddenly, it just 'clicked' at one point. It's hard to put into words…but things are just not the same. And I do feel myself like 'a centre of my world', somehow."

"Good progress!" Sage lifted his eyes from his laptop and greeted Mike with a nod. "The Force is definitely strong with you," he quipped and gestured to the sunbed on his right. "Looks like you're ready to change your vantage point."

"My vantage point?" Mike asked pulling a new stylus tip out of its packaging and replacing the old one. "These things wear out so quickly…" he muttered. "What do you mean?"

"The habit of living out of your ego, and perceiving the world from that perspective. The Buddhists say living from the ego leads to suffering – which it does – but the main point is that it's highly inefficient. Especially in our times."

"Inefficient in what way?"

"Ever heard about 'survival of the fittest'?"

"Of course."

"And how are those 'fittest' different from the rest? What sets them apart?"

"They adapt to the changing environment better. Or faster. Or both."

"That's right," Sage replied. "Here's an important factor that most people are unaware of. To explain what I mean, I have to briefly digress into the topic of time. You see, we exist in time like fish exist in water. It's our habitat, the medium in which we function. We're moulded by it. This is why every generation is different from the ones that came before – they are shaped by a different 'quality' of time."

"Wow! I didn't know that…"

"But apart from the small changes from one decade to the next, there are also large shifts that sweep over entire civilisations – you can see them as 'cosmic seasons'. They happen roughly every two thousand years. They are quite obvious once you know what to look for… They bring massive social changes, new paradigms of thinking, a new dominant religion and such. Notice how much the world has changed over the last two decades," Sage continued nodding at Mike's electronic notepad. "When you were little, such things didn't even exist."

"Hah! You're right."

"The world we live in is light years apart from the world we were born into. Once, it was all about following the rules and doing things the way they had always been done. Getting into a good university to secure a boring-yet-high-paid job with a pension and insurance covered, preferably for life. The 'waste not, want not' and 'the nail that sticks out gets hammered down' type of mentality.

Now, you'll lose the game unless you set up your own business and show your uniqueness, boldly. The winners of the new times are the digital nomads, marketers, ecommers and cryptobros investing in space technologies and flying cars. It's a shocking, radical shift from anything that came before. Can you see that?"

"Wow, yes. When you put it like that."

"You can imagine the new energy of time like a tide rolling in. Whoever goes with the current, will be pushed up to the top. Whoever fails to do so, is going to be crushed or left by the wayside. See how many businesses have rapidly nosedived because they didn't see what was coming? They didn't adjust. It's true on the personal level as well, for personal development. This is what I meant, saying that learning how to function effectively in the new times is a matter of survival."

"Right! I can see it now." Something in Mike's face changed imperceptibly; he looked more focused and intent on catching every word.

"The time when simply being fit and financially successful was enough to thrive, is coming to an end. More and more, the question is about who you *are* as a person, and what you *do*, rather than just what you *have*. These are higher levels of consciousness and awareness we're being pulled into.

The man of the new era is a union of the physical and the divine. We can like the idea or reject it, the flow of time doesn't care. You either catch up or get left behind. It's interesting to see how many people can sense this intuitively. That's why spiritual teachings are becoming more and more mainstream."

"I've noticed that," Mike sniffed. "Many of my friends are into self-development big time."

"Their intuition serves them well," Sage replied. "Becoming a real-life superhero, in other words, a living embodiment of your divine self, is no longer an optional extra. You either do it, or you fail. Because those who've made the right choice will overtake you and leave you in the dust, every time."

"Oh f-ck that! Excuse my language. Not letting it happen. What should I do?"

"Switch your vantage point from your current ego story – 'I'm Mike, a business owner in my thirties, I like this, dislike that, my childhood was such and such' – loosen your attachment to that and learn to show up as your true, Higher Self version instead."

"You mean acting from the top level of the mind?" Mike was pleased to show off that he'd revisited his notes.

"Yes. The upper level of your mind that connects you with pure awareness. A God version of you, in a sense."

Mike rubbed the bridge of his nose. "A God version?"

"The powerful and more evolved version of you that transforms you into a reality bender. Remember that peace and power you felt as pure awareness?"

"Yes."

"You need to activate the level of your mind that can connect you with it, then make it your new vantage point.

Simply speaking, you need to integrate your divine aspect into your life and act from that perspective. This is your God State, or the state of your Higher Self."

"That sounds complicated."

"It isn't. It's only a matter of developing a new thinking habit. Remember, that level of the mind is already a part of you."

"Ah, right."

"The only catch is that it's currently inactive. Most people never get to unlock it... Imagine it like a functional part of your internal 'motherboard', but the connecting wires are all dead. You need to reconnect them, or attach new ones."

"I see."

"For centuries, developing this vantage point was reserved for the chosen few who lived ahead of their time – the saints, the sages and the mystics. But it's no longer so. Now, it's a matter of survival. So you need to make this task a priority."

"Got it."

"Spiritual workout is far from boring, too," Sage narrowed his eyes elvishly. "It's a fascinating adventure. Using your superpowers is a lot of fun. Imagine things effortlessly coming your way. Staying free from distractions, enjoying superhuman motivation, higher levels of energy and drive, and also the ability to heal and fight with energy, if needed.

Bending reality to create the best life for yourself and others who matter. Feeling empowered and in control, without struggling for it.

And the ability to see ahead through intuition and clairvoyance, to influence, lead and impact more. These are great advantages in life."

"Sounds great for sure," Mike nodded with a downward curve of his lips, imagining the possibilities.

"Just like with any new habit, you'll need consistency to start with. But once you get there, you'll be wondering why would you ever not live in that state. It's incredible. Only by embracing your God state, can you fully experience true inner peace and flow, as well as a sense of freedom and personal power. This is what it truly means to 'live as designed'."

"How do I get there?" Mike swirled the stylus in his fingers.

"Have a look at this chart first, it will help you remember this visually," Sage opened his laptop and turned the screen to Mike.

LEVELS OF CONSCIOUSNESS

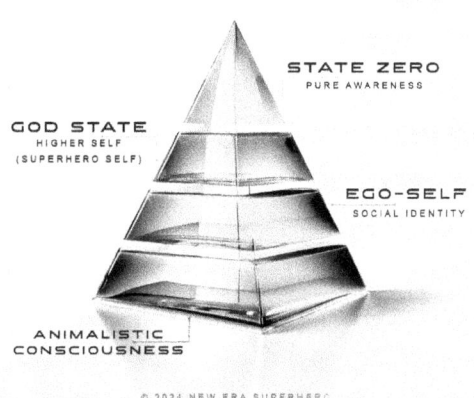

"Wow, that's the prettiest chart I've seen in a while," Mike commented.

"Why, thank you. My friend Stable Diffusion and I are both flattered," Sage replied jokingly.

Mike flashed his eyebrows. "You know about AI?"

"I know about lots of things," Sage smiled a magician smile. "Remember, one must always be aligned with the current of time."

"Huh, must be weird for someone who lived in ancient cities…"

"It is a bit, but not too much. I lived in other places, too," Sage's gaze took on a distant cast for a moment. "But let's get back to the point."

"Yes! So what are the steps?"

"Alright, let's begin. First, sit with your back straight," Sage instructed. "Start with the full body relaxation – the medi warmup. Pull your shoulders down to the ground…then release them. Now tense and relax your hands…and go through the rest of the steps. I trust you remember them by now."

Mike responded with a nod.

"Good. Now bring your attention to your body. Notice its sitting position, the way it's breathing, and any other sensations you may pick up. Simply observe them for a bit. This is to anchor you in the alpha brainwaves."

Mike nodded again.

"Now, focus on both wrists at the same time, as before. If thoughts or feelings come up, simply observe them with no involvement. Soon, they will fade.

Alright, good.

Now, focus on the silence between thoughts. Allow yourself to experience your *being*, existing in this moment, with no beginning and no end. Just one eternal now. Let go of all concerns, worries, and memories – right now, there's nowhere you need to be, and nothing you need to do except simply *being*.

Now, from that silence, imagine that your most powerful and divine self is standing there in front of you. Don't try to picture anything specific – simply allow the vision to appear. Give it a little bit of time, if needed.

Alright.

Now, let that vision come forward and merge with you. Notice how that feels. Go into full exploration mode. Find out how you'd feel about yourself as your divine version. How would you see the world?

 Where would you want to live? What fashion style would you wear, and how would you speak? How would you respond to things and make decisions as your divine self? Who would you choose to be in your life?

Give yourself time. Don't rush anything.

Allow your visions to flow freely. Observe, absorb.

Experience the sense of your divine self fully. Make yourself at home in this new state.

Take your time.

Then, when you feel ready, you can choose to come back. Say to yourself that the clarity and your sense of power and completeness will remain with you even as you come out of this meditation.

Slowly, start bringing your attention to your breathing again. Allow your breath to carry you back to this time and this place. Yes, just like so.

And when you're ready to return, wiggle your fingers and your toes, and finish with a stretch to realign yourself fully."

Mike did as instructed, then slowly opened his eyes.

"Now, look at your bracelet," Sage said. "And mentally anchor your state on it. Every time you forget who you are, simply look at your bracelet, and it will help you remember."

Mike nodded silently, contemplating his surroundings with a deep and lucid gaze. He somehow seemed taller. And younger.

"I can see a glow around everything," he said finally. "Mostly blue. Around all objects. But around you, it's gold. What is this?"

"The aura," Sage told him. "There's a condensed field of the Light, or Force, around everything. Once you learn to perceive reality as it is, you start seeing it."

"Gotcha," Mike responded pensively, studying the patio as

though he was seeing it for the first time. He lifted his hand and turned it around in front of his face. "How strange. So it was there, all along? This is what the world actually looks like?"

"One of its levels, yes. This ability is called Extended Perception. It will be very useful for you going forward. The more you develop it, the more you'll be able to see other people for who they *really* are. Which is invaluable both in business and when choosing a life partner, too."

"For sure. It's getting fainter, though? The glow."

"It's normal for the first time. Your mind is trying to bring back its default mode. With a bit of practice, you'll learn to use this perception at will. Tell me, how do you feel right now?"

"Good question." Mike lapsed into silence looking for words, but then a corner of his mouth curved in a smile. "I feel… powerful. In a strange way that I don't know how to describe. Complete. Free. Unstoppable. Inspired. I mean, inspired to do great things. Like, *really* great things."

"Change the course of human civilisation?" Sage teased him.

"Maybe," Mike smirked. "That one definitely needs some work." He paused and rubbed his chin thoughtfully. "It's a bizarre feeling, in a way. It feels like being invincible. And expansive. Like a long-forgotten feeling I had once known, but lost since. And now it's back. A sense that I belong… like being at home, being *fully me*. It's great." He felt a little tingling running through his body as he spoke. "And the emptiness is gone!" He added a sense of relief.

"The emptiness?"

"Well," Mike grimaced slightly and glanced away. "I never talked to anyone about it. But it haunted me, kinda always. You know what they say that making lots of money is gonna make you feel good about yourself? Well, it didn't quite work for me. In fact, the better my business was doing, the worse it got, in a way. Sometimes I felt like a fraud, even though I wasn't. I *hated* that.

I went to some confidence workshops, some famous ones. Tried all their stuff. But it was like putting on a mask." Mike rubbed his face. "Deep down, there was this nasty little voice saying, 'Nah, that's not enough. You're no good. What are you doing with your life?' And it felt…empty. No matter what I did, or how much I had, it felt like always missing the mark, somehow. And now… Finally! I don't feel it anymore. Wow. This alone made my training with you worth it." Mike took a deep breath. "Thank you. I mean, it's not the only win, but it's a game-changer for me. I hated that damn feeling."

"That voice came from the ego," Sage told him. "And now, as you've learnt to go beyond, the ego's worldview is no longer valid. This is what I meant when I said you'd have to leave your previous life behind.

Your ego doesn't know who you really are, and so the life it had created didn't reflect you as a person. That's one of the main reasons why it felt empty and stifling. It was 'too small' for you. But now, you have the freedom to show up fully, and to start living a life you'll be inspired to live."

"That sounds awesome." Mike leant back on his sunbed, threw his hands behind his head and looked up to the sky. "What about my superpowers?" He squinted roguishly.

"That's the practical training part, your 'flying lessons'," Sage replied. "We'll do it once we finish the theory. But not straight away. First, go back home, give yourself time to think things over and integrate what you've learnt. Then, when you're ready, reach out and we'll plan our next steps." He paused. "For you, I'd suggest training in Bali."

"Why Bali?"

"Different places have different energy. I always choose the one that best supports the student's goals."

"I see. Where else do you go?"

"Depends. I travel the world a lot. Bali, Japan, Italy, Costa Rica, Nepal… I went a few times to Iceland as well. And the Dubai desert. Different people need different training conditions. This part is more structured. It's a bit of a Shaolin-like 'teacher-student' kind of training."

"That sounds fascinating… Look forward to it." Mike focused on his breathing – deep and even – trying to make the otherworldly lucidity stay. "Living like this all the time would be awesome."

"It gets better from there," Sage smiled. "You'll see. But first, here's something else I want to share."

"I'm all ears," Mike picked up his notepad again, contemplating how addictive his current peace of mind was.

"Did you ever try to use Midjourney when it first came out?" Sage asked out of the blue.

Mike blinked at him, confused. "The AI service that creates pictures from words?"

"Yes."

"Uhm, yeah. I did give it a go. Why?"

"How impressed were you with the accuracy of those

pictures?"

"Well…" Mike chucked remembering eight-fingered hands coming out of the chests, torsos twisted into knots and other 'wonders'. "Moderately."

"So the result was somewhat along the lines of what you had described. Enough to recognise the prompt, but a far cry from what it should have been."

"Yes."

"Well, this is roughly how your ego 'renders' your true divine self."

Mike snorted. "No way, that's hilarious."

"From the perspective of your Higher Self – totally. But people who make those distorted visions of self their core identity, get trapped in very unsatisfying lives. The ego doesn't have the resources to allow for us to 'live as designed'. It's not good enough, and it knows that. That's why living from the level of the ego leads to pain."

"Hmm, I can see that," Mike smiled ironically. "From experience."

"Your God State is where you truly belong."

"Alright. I'm curious, though. Speaking of the God State…" Mike twirled the stylus in his fingers, "where does the actual God come into the picture?"

"Depends what you mean by the actual God."

"You know, the Creator. The Almighty. The Higher Principle."

"You got in touch with that Higher Principle when you entered the state of pure awareness," Sage said.

"Hmm?"

"It is the Source. All Creation flows from there. God's consciousness permeates the entire universe, everything you see and can't see. It is what makes up the fabric of the Universe on the fundamental level. The idea of 'all is one' comes from there."

"No, I mean how does it fit with Christianity, for example? That's the faith I was brought up with."

Sage smiled lightly. "All truths converge. If you recall, the Gospel of John says, 'In the beginning was the Word, and the Word was with God, and the Word was God. All things were made by him; and without him was not any thing made that was made." The 'Word' is the initial impulse of Creation, coming from God and being God, reverberating through all that is.'

Mike looked at Sage astounded. "You know the Bible by heart?"

Sage smiled again. "Some of it, I do."

"Wow, never expected that. So you're religious yourself?"

"Not in the usual sense, I'm not," Sage answered mildly. "But the Bible is a very profound book if you read it right. Besides, knowing that everything, including you, is made of the energy of the Source – the Light – God – the Force or whatever you want to call it – it's simply logical to operate from that perspective."

"Makes sense. But what about God-like people like Jesus?"

"He's an example of what's possible. The more you get aligned with your Higher Self, the greater influence you get on the fabric of reality. Jesus didn't actually speak of himself as God, but rather emphasised the Higher Consciousness being our inherent nature. Remember what he said? 'Ye are gods; and all of you are children of the Most High.' God's consciousness is waiting to be awakened within each human being. The core of living our Purpose is to unlock that dormant power and let it flow through us."

"Wow, that's something really inspiring to think about."

"You see, 'aligning yourself with God' is simply striving to align with your inherent nature, which would empower and illuminate your life. It's a smart choice for anyone who doesn't want to waste their time here. Think about it this way – since we're stuck on this planet for a while, we may as well make the most of it. And – all other things being equal – a life of meaning, flow and boundless creativity is better than being stuck feeling anxious and empty. If you have an option to upgrade your ride, why not take it." Sage took a jug of hydrogen water from his side table, poured two glasses, and offered one to Mike.

"Thank you," Mike reached out to grab his glass. "You talk about it as though it's something automatic, though."

"In a way, it is. The closer you get to your real nature, the more your mind gets calm, joyful and lucid. It's just a hallmark of living as your true self, beyond the ego."

"Is it really that simple?"

"It's straightforward enough. You'll need some persistence, as I said before, and a better understanding of how the Light's – God's – energy works. From there, you'll naturally start taking powerful and aligned actions, so you can create your greatest life and impact. Consistency must come from within," he smiled briefly. "And the techniques to bend reality you'll learn during our practical training."

"That sounds very clear and achievable. Love it." Mike emptied his glass and flashed a broad smile. "Can't wait to start."

Mike's homework notes:

"Get more familiar with State Zero (the pure awareness state), but keep the sessions short."

"Meditate on merging with my Higher Self and perceiving the world from that perspective.

- How would I see the world as my divine self?

- Where would I want to live?

- What would I be excited about?

- What would my fashion style and speaking style be like?

- What would I do differently?

Note: rethink who I want in my close social circle."

"Generate an image of my Higher Self for inspiration and keep it on my phone."

CHAPTER 17: DESIGNING A PERSONAL MANIFESTO

"The privilege of a lifetime is to become who you truly are."
–Carl Gustav Jung

"To make your vision for your best life real, you must first make the best version of yourself real. Design it like you'd design your character in a game. Start by writing down the qualities, priorities and attributes that he has. Pay special attention to the qualities and values that your current version may not have, or not have developed fully. Remember to include your divine aspect."

"Ironic," Mike said to Sage when they met again. He looked down and contemplated his clasped hands for a moment. "I must admit, I wasn't fully honest with you. Or with myself, for that matter. Sorry. I've been roleplaying for so long that I seem to have forgotten. And yet," he lifted his gaze and a dangerous smile briefly touched his lips, "part of me had always known. I just refused to listen."

Sage looked at him, his eyes narrow with amusement, but his gaze was warm and kind. He remained silent, waiting for Mike to finish.

Mike sighed and shook his head. "Imagine being drunk and really cringey but you don't realise how cringey you are because you're drunk?" He snorted. "That's the story of my life." He paused and then continued, "I pretended I was surprised when you showed me that energy stuff…because I guess I was conditioned to respond that way. But really, I've known it since I was a kid. Back then, I could see that glow around things. Then I lost the ability over the years.

I've always been different from other kids. I could sense people's emotions, and even predict what they would say or do in the next moment. Sometimes, I'd see a dream and then it happened in real life exactly like that. It was cool but also… frightening in a way, you know?

I started thinking what else could have been possible, and then shied away from it because I didn't know how to handle that.

And so started living as a roleplayer. I watched what others did – like the men I regarded to be cool and powerful, and copied that. I followed their blueprint and succeeded, much in the way they did.

But deep down, it always felt frustrating. Like as if I was secretly angry all the time. And I guess I was. With myself and my choices. Seeing my life slipping by and not even having the courage to face it as *me*." Mike pressed his lips together. "I was even mocking people who did this spiritual stuff because I heard others saying so. I was trying to resist it too, as you remember. Not because I disagreed with it…but out of fear.

Hearing about it stirred up all those demons from childhood. And also the sense of shame – of being different, worse. Like there was something wrong with me. I had almost no friends growing up. I later learnt how to act to get on with the 'cool kids'. I was popular in college, even. I was proud of myself to have created a persona others liked." Mike winced and took a long breath. He couldn't remember the last time he spoke to someone so openly. The freedom to finally do it was surprisingly liberating.

"So I meditated and suddenly saw my life up to this point – a fearful shadow of a man, following other's ideas, trying to fit in. And realised how pathetic it has been. Like, deeply, in my heart. Beyond words. I felt so angry for that wasted time that it actually… it kinda…damn. It made me emotional for a moment." He winced again and rubbed the bridge of his nose. "I mean, what an idiot…"

Mike paused again then looked at Sage. His gaze was sharp and lucid. "Thank you," he said. "Thank you for helping me remember. In meditation, I… I saw a different version of my life, the one where I never woke up. It was awful. Soul-destroying. A 'muggle' life. I couldn't…wouldn't be able to live like that. And it was such a near miss. So, thank you." He closed his eyes as the dark vision flashed through his mind. Mike dismissed it at once, and brought his focus back to the present moment.

He ran his fingers through his hair then fixed his gaze on Sage again and smiled – the smile of a tired traveller that finally returned home. "I can do what you do. Look," he said stretching his hand out in front of him. "I've figured it out. Might be hard to see in the sunlight…" A ball of glowing energy, hardly visible, danced above his open palm. "It's going to be hilarious," he continued meditatively, folding his hands and resting them on his lap, "when people find out that they had never actually known me for who I am. All these years. Ironic." He snorted. "Don't remember ever talking so much."

Mike finished and lapsed into silence thinking of a path that was unfolding before him. Eventually, he flopped his back on the sunbed and threw his hands behind his head. "So, what's the plan?"

"Well, first of all, congratulations. And welcome back," Sage said with a smile.

"What do you mean, welcome back?"

"The real you."

"Oh. I see," Mike paused. "You mean, you knew all along?"

"Of course," Sage smiled again. "That's how I know who's ready to become a student. I see people for who they really are. You'll need that skill as well. I'll teach you at our training in

Bali."

"Extended perception?"

"Yes. That's what all real-life superheroes use. It's a crucial ability to have if you want to thrive in our fast-changing times."

"I can see that. Look forward to learning it."

"Plenty of otherworldly fun awaits you," Sage said. "But before you get to that second stage, you'll need a new Personal Manifesto that is aligned with your soul's path. You can see it as your personal mission statement. A description of who you are and what you bring into the world. In other words, what your greatest service is."

"Hold on... That exercise I tried to do earlier? But I couldn't make it work."

"This time, you will," Sage smiled lightly. "You've unlocked the right perspective to succeed with it now. It will serve as your mental foundation as you progress, your anchor."

"My anchor?"

"Yes. Your actions, thoughts, choices, and the way you feel about yourself are all rooted in your *identity,* in who you see yourself as. This is why creating the right identity is key to starting to live your Purpose. Do you see how it works?"

"Yes."

"I'm going to share with you a set of questions for self-assessment. It consists of two parts, as you may remember from before. You'll need to keep a journal for this. First, you need to get clarity on your starting point where you're currently at. Write things exactly as they are right now. Then, you'll add the destination parameters – the description for your greatest future self. I'm going to explain how to do that in a moment.

The mind works somewhat like a satnav. If you give it a clear starting point and a clear goal to reach, it will start calculating routes to take you there. Most people are stuck in limbo because they have a fuzzy concept of who they are, and an even more vague idea of the type of life that would make them feel fulfilled." Sage paused. "Another reason why you want to start from your current position is because it will give you a reference point of what feels true and what doesn't. So that when you're writing about your future, you can use that feeling for guidance."

"Got it."

"Great. Here are the questions for part one:

1. What do you bring to other people's lives? What's it like to have you as a friend? As a partner? A team or a family member? A boss? An employee?

2. Have you consciously chosen your path (i.e. Are you doing what you want to do, going where you want to go and becoming who you want to become) or are you doing your work to prove yourself to other people?

3. How do you feel when you do what you do? What does your body tell you? What does your conscience/soul tell you?

4. Take a look at what your life currently represents. This

includes your business, your level of income, your type of clients and your lifestyle. These results will show your main priorities in life and your beliefs about yourself and the world.

Based on what are your life shows, what your core beliefs, limitations and priorities?

5. List the priorities you discovered above in order of importance. Keep in mind these priorities can be both positive and negative: i.e. a positive priority is to 'stay healthy' while a negative priority could be 'to play safe' or 'to receive other people's approval even at the cost of compromising your true desires'. Negative priorities are as valid as positive ones.

6. What dominant conversation do you have with yourself daily? E.g. "I'm an impostor", "I can do anything I put my mind to", "I'm an achiever type," "I suck at expressing myself," "Life is meant to be hard", etc. Your mind is taking you in the direction of your dominant thoughts every second of every day. Do you like the destination you're heading towards?

7. What environment/circumstances bring out the best of you? (When you feel motivated, inspired and fired up to achieve great things).

8. What environment/circumstances bring out the worst of you? (When you feel disempowered, defeated and apathetic).

9. Do you have an idea of how much money you need to make your greatest life's vision a reality? If so, write it down.

10. What business avenue/project/opportunity secretly excites you but you wouldn't dare to go anywhere near it?

11. What are the top 3 activities you need no accountability for because you're naturally organised and inspired to do them? They must be related to self-development or self-expression (for example, learning about something specific, doing creative work or levelling up physically and mentally in some way.)

12. What topics do you like reading, watching, or talking about the most?

13. What are your 5 core values in life? (These are your non-negotiables – things that you feel must be present in your life/character no matter what. List them in order of importance.)

14. What did you dream about as a child? Who did you imagine yourself to become? (Include any fantasy world answers, too.)

15. What are your natural gifts? (These are things you're good at, and excited about, but you may not have the opportunity to use them in your current circumstances. You may also think that they are 'weird', 'way out there', 'nobody is going to be interested in this', or

even 'shameful' – even though they are not objectively immoral.)

16. What is one decision you can make today to take you from your current results to success and a sense of happiness and fulfilment?

17. What do you never get tired of learning about or practising, and would love to become extraordinarily good at?

18. What do you feel the most anger towards? Why?

19. What is the actual, deeper why behind your answer to p.18?

20. What do you feel the most love and excitement towards? Why?

21. What is the actual, deeper why behind your answer to p.20?

22. If money considerations didn't exist and circumstances allowed, what would you be doing today that would make your life more meaningful and exciting? What would make your soul sing?

"To get the most out of this exercise you must approach it with respect and radical honesty. Give yourself as much time as you need. Remember, you don't need pretty answers, only the true ones. Be prepared that some discoveries can make you feel hurt or emotional – allow those emotions to come up. They are part of the clearing-out process. Keep your answers private, of course."

"Will do. And what's the second part?"

"Get into your God State like I taught you, and sit with it for a while. When you feel ready, ask yourself these questions–"

1. What kind of person would you become if you didn't place superimposed psychological limitations on yourself coming from your background, parents or environment?

2. What do you bring to other people's lives as your most elite self? What's it like to have you as a friend? As a partner? A boss? An employee?

3. How do you feel when you do what you do as your Higher Self? What does your body tell you? What does your conscience/soul tell you?

4. Visualise your best life, a life that would be truly worth living. How would your perfect life *feel*? (The marker of the right vision is an instant sense of relief, liberation and expansiveness.)

5. What would you have achieved in an ideal world that would give you a sense of completion and fulfilment? (i.e. The sense of fully expressing yourself as a human being, and giving the world your greatest service and gifts. What would your most inspiring legacy be?)

6. Thinking of your greatest vision for your business, what will be your impact on other people? How will your work make them feel? How is it going to affect their

lives?

7. What is your level of income, your type of clients and your lifestyle aligned with your Higher Self?

8. What kind of priorities and in what order does that elite version of you have, to make this version of reality possible?

9. What environment/activities/circumstances bring out the best of you? (When you feel motivated, inspired and fired up to achieve great things).

10. What environment/activities/circumstances bring you down? (When you feel disconnected from your core, defeated and apathetic)

11. What are your 5 core values in life from the position of your Higher Self? (These are your non-negotiables – things that you feel must be present in your life/character no matter what. List them in order of importance.)

12. What is the big message you want to spread that is more important than your business or your work?

"As before, take your time with these. Don't try to complete the whole list in one sitting. It's the quality of the answers and not the speed that matters. Finding out the true answers to the questions above could be the most important and life-changing work you've ever done for your self-development."

"Everything has been pretty life-changing so far," Mike

smiled picking up his glass of orange juice.

"That's…why I'm here," Sage answered humorously. "Is everything clear so far?"

"Yes."

"Great. Once you've completed both parts of your self-audit, you can start designing your Personal Manifesto based on the information you've uncovered. This part is really creative and fun. It will help you to solidify the new concept of self and also to bridge the gap between your current life and the greatest vision you would like to live. That manifesto is a set of statements that you will need to incorporate into your mindset."

"Like affirmations?"

"No, not like that. You can think of them as lines of code you want to add to your subconscious programming. You can only say them to yourself during the day once they're 'successfully installed' and feel fully congruent. But first, you need to install them correctly to make them work."

"How do I do that?"

"I'm going to explain it in a moment. First, have a look at these. Here are some ideas you can use for inspiration." Sage turned his laptop screen towards Mike so he could read the list. " Choose anything that resonates, and then add your own."

***

I can achieve anything I commit to

I'm a natural-born winner

I'm a recognised creator of…

Being fulfilled and successful is my birthright

My presence is magnetic

My presence inspires others

I earn greatly so I can serve greatly

I'm a master of my reality, the sun around which my entire world rotates

I am manifested power of God/the Light

Every day, I confidently progress towards my goals

I'm the best in the world at what I do

People respect and appreciate my input and my work

I have outstanding intuition and analytical abilities

My success is inevitable

***

"As you might have guessed, these are pointers for the ego mind to give it clarity of focus," Sage added. "Your Higher Self already has all these qualities. As your process of evolving towards that state continues, you'll find that there's no need to remind yourself or meditate on them. They will become something that goes without saying, just like you don't affirm what colour your eyes are."

"Got it."

"Here is how to 'install' these ideas so that they get accepted by your subconscious mind:

Choose times during the day when your brain goes into alpha, or even slower, theta brainwaves. For most people, these are the moments right before they fall asleep and just after they wake up. This is why the first 15 minutes at the beginning and the end of the day are the most important... But any trance-like state – say, meditation, relaxing on the beach or nature-watching – works as well.

That cosy feeling on the brink of falling asleep is a gateway to your subconscious. Once you sense you've reached that state, choose a line from the list and start contemplating it as a concept. Imagine what it would be like to live in alignment with that quality.

What it would mean for yourself and others.

What kind of mindset it would naturally create.

What kind of life you'd be living based on that.

Vividly imagine situations that would confirm that quality in you, or present the opportunities for it to shine. Focus on how others are responding, and what *feeling* it gives you. Play those scenes in your mind over and over, gradually speeding them up until the visuals and sounds become a blur – and only the background feeling remains. Focus on maximising that feeling and allow yourself to drift to sleep with it.

Once you feel naturally drawn to act on that chosen quality in your waking life, move on to the next. Don't worry if your efforts don't seem 'perfect' to begin with, just keep going. Every experience counts.

Step by step, assemble your new Personal Manifesto out of these concepts strung together.

Once you've designed your new story, 'live through it' in a meditation. Visualise living as your future self, now. See all the events unfolding as you intended them to unfold. See the right people entering your life. The right opportunities appear. And all the while, notice how it makes you *feel*.

Anchor that feeling and bring it up during your waking hours, as often as you can. Learn to make decisions and choices that are aligned with it.

It also helps to think about what your future self would wear, how he would move and talk. Introduce some of that future style and those mannerisms into your current life. Don't be too hung up on that part, though. If you're doing your meditation practice right, these things will evolve naturally. But being mindful of them helps to speed up the process."

"Got it. I'm curious though, why did you emphasise the feeling part?"

"This is what you need to bring your visualisation to life. You see, for your mind, there's no difference between an actual memory and something that you vividly imagine…as long as you add emotions to the mix.

Your emotional baseline, which produces your dominant thoughts about yourself and what's possible for you, needs to be reset to match your goals. This is how people who come from humble backgrounds can get to the top by rewriting the way they feel about themselves. There are plenty of such examples.

The brain likes repeating set, familiar patterns. Whether it's a track record of successes or a track record of failures, it will do its best to deliver more of the same. So if your past doesn't have the relevant 'experience log', your task is to create it using visualisation and 'install' those experiences yourself."

"A bit like 'fake it till you make it' attitude?"

"No," Sage frowned slightly. "You must not *fake it*. Play that new Personal Manifesto movie in your mind over and over, until your subconscious accepts it as true; even though in your current circumstances it can be a bit of an isekai – 'a truth misplaced in time'.

However, you must know that because you're the master of your reality, your 'future truth' is real and valid, and it's on its way, even though you haven't seen it yet.

Think of it like this: imagine someone owes you a payment. They texted you to let you know they put it through, and sent you a confirmation screenshot. The transfer took place through a traditional bank over a weekend, so you won't see the money in your account until a few days later. Relatable?"

"Hah, totally."

"Now, even though you don't see the funds on your bank statement yet, you know it's already yours because it's already on its way. The arrival is simply a matter of time. So you have a sense of certainty."

"Yes."

"Well, that same sense of certainty is what you need to maintain while waiting for your best reality to be 'delivered'. Once you've designed it and put your mental settings right – in other words, adjusted your emotional baseline to match the frequency of your desired life – you must be certain that it's already on its way. Doubts will slow the process down."

"Got it."

"One last hack – if you want to turbocharge the speed, create that vision from the viewpoint of your Higher Self. Simply enter your God State first and *then* meditate on your desired vision of yourself and your greatest life."

"Fantastic, I'll do that."

"Your ultimate goal is to live your life as your *true self*, that is, your God State self. Getting there takes time, though. Allow yourself to grow at your own pace. Your Personal Manifesto will be your guiding thread while doing the work."

"Got it. How long such should a manifesto be, by the way?"

"It's best to keep it short enough to be able to easily remember it. But if you prefer, you can write it out in your journal as well, and read it every morning and every evening, using the programming technique above. Always phrase your sentences in the present tense, for example, "I am", "I have,", "I do" and so on. Your subconscious can only relate to the present moment."

"Understood."

"Here's one more thing that will help you channel your God State into your everyday life. Become radically aware of your strengths, abilities and talents. Learn to notice and appreciate sincerely the good things in you, the traits that you're proud of, in a non-selfish way. Find out what qualities you have that you would admire in someone else. Let your mind dwell on those qualities as part of your contribution to the world. Have you considered them before?"

"That's a really good point," Mike replied while finishing his notes. "I don't think I have. I tend to notice my shortcomings more."

"This is a typical focus for the ego-mind. Your Higher Self is more in sync with your potential than your shadows. The point of this exercise is not to make you oblivious of the areas that still need some work, by the way. It is to shift your focus away from your ego and towards your greatest expression as a human being. To help you become as aware of your potential as you are of your perceived flaws."

"Sounds great. Will start working on this ASAP." Mike looked at the sky tinted with afternoon hues. He wondered how long it would take to complete the assignment.

"This shouldn't take you too long," Sage replied as though answering his thoughts. "Reach out on Telegram when you're ready."

"Can't wait to learn to use my superpowers," Mike smiled but then his face took on a pensive cast. "So much to unpack and think about. Feels kind of weird going back, though." He slowly closed the cover of his notepad. "That was a mind-blowing journey, I must say. It really was."

"It's not over yet," Sage's voice sounded like an invitation to a new adventure. "You'll love the second part even more, you'll see."

"That sounds awesome. Look forward to it." Mike said. He suddenly thought of Luke and smirked briefly. *Luke will be envious as hell.* Finally, he sighed, decisively put his notepad in his bag, zipped it, and got up. "Well," he said. "Thank you."

"Take care, and keep in touch," Sage told him warmly.

"Will do." Mike flashed a broad smile then suddenly touched his temple with the flair of a military salute. "Can't wait to continue our training."

He turned to walk away; the late afternoon sun painted his hair all gold.

The future looked exciting.

AFTERWORD

I hope this book has been an enjoyable and insightful companion on your personal growth journey. I will be glad if it serves its purpose to become a stepping stone towards your most meaningful and exciting life.

I hope it inspired you to unlock your master vision, to dream bigger and to dare and serve greatly.

I'd love to hear about your results and any questions you may have. You can connect with me at reachout@newerasuperhero.com. t

Feel free to pass this book on to any friend or a team member who would also benefit from it.

And if you're inspired to experience training similar to what Mike had, you can start by booking your free assessment interview below.

https://newerasuperhero.com/calendar

ONE LAST THING

You're a hero to have made it this far!

Here's one last thing…

I wrote this book to help others – people just like you. I hope you enjoyed reading this and found value, insight and inspiration within these pages. If so, I'd be honoured if you would consider joining me on my quest to help spread the word by leaving an Amazon review.

Every voice counts!

Your review would stir up Amazon's algorithm, boosting the book's ranking and visibility, and help it to be discovered by new readers. And that would make me very happy. :)

If you've also taken any of my courses, feel free to mention them in your review as well.

Thank you!

ABOUT THE AUTHOR
New Era Superhero: Self-Mastery & Service

▼World-Class Spiritual Evolution for Mission-Driven Men◢

Jay H. Tepley is an author, entrepreneur, international speaker and spiritual mentor. A lifelong geek and a dedicated researcher, she offers world-class personal evolution training for A-players in marketing, coaching and community building to help them fly high and achieve beyond what other people think possible.

Over the last 20 years, her New Era Superhero program showed many men across the globe the path to increased revenue, success, impact, and personal fulfilment by helping them connect with their soul Purpose.

Her charity work supporting mental health through lightsaber training has been featured in the Guardian, The Sunday Times Radio, The Jeremy Vine Show and BBC 1.

When she's not teaching or writing, Jay enjoys reading about Japan where she studied and lived for a time (she speaks fluent Japanese, and her unique novel, the Lightwatch Chronicles, begins in Tokyo).

You can connect with Jay as well as find other resources including her books, audiobooks, meditations, videos, courses and life events announcements in a dedicated Telegram channel here:

https://t.me/NewEraSuperhero

If you feel ready to take your life to a new level, you can book your free interview below to be considered for personal mentorship:

https://www.newerasuperhero.com/calendar

It could be the start of an incredible journey. Fly high!

For any other queries, interviews, podcast and TV appearances or speaker requests, please get in touch at reachout@ NewEraSuperhero.com.

GET SOCIAL!

Join our stellar community here:

Website: http://www.NewEraSuperhero.com

Telegram: https://t.me/NewEraSuperhero

YouTube: @NewEraSuperhero

Instagram: @NewEraSuperhero

Facebook: @NewEraSuperhero

TikTok: @NewEraSuperhero

You can also enquire about **joining our Superhero's Training League** at
https://join.newerasuperhero.com

Join us and:

» Meet like-minded entrepreneurs and trailblazers

» Speed up your progress through monthly training calls

» Unlimited access to students-only discussion hub for networking, questions and accountability

» Unlimited access to the most comprehensive spiritual and self-development library for men, with many exclusive training videos and materials

» Learn how to become the more elite version of you and align with your Purpose in the shortest time possible, create an epic legacy and serve the world greatly

THE SUPERHERO'S JOURNEY